PENGUIN BOOKS

ESSENTIAL CHINESE (Mandarin)

Also published in this series:

Essential Arabic
Essential Japanese

GW00722694

ESSENTIAL CHINESE
(*Mandarin*)

A Guidebook to Language and Culture

COMPILED BY LEXUS
with Michael Dillon, Li Kaining
and Catharine Sanders

PENGUIN BOOKS

PENGUIN BOOKS

Published by the Penguin Group
27 Wrights Lane, London W8 5TZ, England
Viking Penguin Inc., 40 West 23rd Street, New York, New York 10010, USA
Penguin Books Australia Ltd, Ringwood, Victoria, Australia
Penguin Books Canada Ltd, 2801 John Street, Markham, Ontario,
Canada L3R 1B4
Penguin Books (NZ) Ltd, 182–190 Wairau Road, Auckland 10, New Zealand

Penguin Books Ltd, Registered Offices: Harmondsworth, Middlesex, England

First published 1990
1 3 5 7 9 10 8 6 4 2

Copyright © Lexus Ltd, 1990
All rights reserved

Filmset in Linotron Plantin Light
Made and printed in Great Britain by
Cox & Wyman Ltd, Reading

CONTENTS

INTRODUCTION

This is a guidebook to Chinese language and culture. Information is presented in one single A–Z listing in which dictionary and phrasebook elements are interwoven with descriptive passages on language, grammar and culture.

The dictionary/phrasebook elements give a vocabulary of some 1,500 everyday words and expressions, providing an excellent basis for self-expression in the foreign language.

The Chinese words and expressions are presented in a form known as Pinyin, which uses the Roman alphabet. To this has been added a pronunciation guide so that the Chinese words and expressions can easily be read out (see also the notes on pronunciation on page ix).

The language and grammar notes provide explanations of how the Chinese language works. If you want to go a little further, these sections will enable you to develop some basic skills with the Chinese language and to develop a knowledge of its structure.

More language notes and some useful expressions are given within the culture note sections: typical polite expressions, for example, what to say in specific circumstances, how to address people etc. – all valuable language tips for the traveller.

The culture notes and cross-cultural comparisons cover a wide range of topics – from the Chinese calendar to food, from public holidays to foreign exchange certificates, from bicycles to toilets – all having the same purpose of acting as a guide to a country that is not just foreign but different.

This book can operate at various levels. You can use it as a kind of travel book, to be read at home; you can take it abroad with you and use it as a dictionary/phrasebook; you can use it as an introduction to the Chinese language; or you can simply dip into it as a source of information about another civilization.

NOTES ON PRONUNCIATION

Tones

Chinese is a tonal language. This means basically that words can be spoken with four types of intonation: a level intonation (ˉ), a rising intonation (ˊ), a falling and rising intonation (ˇ) or a falling intonation (ˋ). Sometimes a word represented by the same letters in Pinyin will vary in meaning according to its tonal pattern. For more details on this see the entry TONES. In general, you would be well advised to ask a Chinese to give you an aural demonstration of the difference between the tones.

Pinyin

Translations in this book are given in Pinyin. For more on this see the entry PINYIN. As you will soon discover, Pinyin is not a pronunciation system. So we have added a special feature in this book: a pronunciation guide which writes out the Pinyin as though it were English. So, if you read the pronunciation guide as though it were English *and* follow the tone marks as given in the translations you should be able to communicate with a Chinese. Some notes on this pronunciation guide:

ai	as in 'Thailand'
ay	as in 'way'
ee	as in 'feet'
ew	as in 'dew' (better: as in French 'du')
g	is always hard as in 'go' or 'girl'
I	as in 'I' or the 'i' in 'China'
j	as in 'Janet'
oo	as in 'soon'
ow	as in 'cow'
un	as the 'an' in 'balance' or the 'en' in 'open'
ur	as in 'fur'
y	is always as in 'you', never as in 'why'

Since Pinyin uses English letters in a special way, the following conversion table may be of use:

c	ts
q	ch
x	sh
zh	j (as in 'Janet')
ai	as in 'Thai'
ao	as in 'now' or 'Mao'
e	as in 'her'
ei	as in 'weight'
en	as in 'open'
eng	with the 'e' as in 'her'
i	either as in 'Maria' or if coming after c, ch, r, s, sh, z, zh then like the 'i' sound in 'sir'
ia	like the 'ya' in 'yard'
ie	like the 'ye' in 'yellow'
iu	like the 'yo' in 'yo-yo'
o	as in 'for'
ou	as in 'Joe' or 'dough'
ong	with the 'o' as in 'who'
u	either as in 'soon' or if coming after j, q, x then like the 'u' sound in French 'du' or German 'über'
ü	as in French 'du' or German 'über'
ua, uai	with the 'u' like 'w'
ui	as in 'way'
uo	as in 'war'

A

a, an

There are no words in Chinese corresponding to 'a' and 'an'. You just use the noun by itself. For example:

qìchē [chee-cher] a car
háizi [hI-dzur] a child
yāoqǐng [yow-ching] an invitation

So if, for example, you want to ask for a cup of coffee, you say:

I would like a cup of coffee
wó xiǎng hē bēi kāfēi
[wor syahng her bay kah-fay]

which means literally:

I like drink cup coffee

Or if you want to ask for a map of Shanghai you say:

have you a map of Shanghai?
ní yǒu Shànghǎi dìtú ma?
[nee yoh shahng-hI dee-too mah]

which means literally:

you have Shanghai map (*question word*)?

The word for 'one' – **yī** – can sometimes be used to convey the sense of 'a' or 'an':

yíge Zhōngguo ren
[yee-ger joong-gwor run]
a Chinese person

But this usually happens when it is necessary to point out that only one object is being referred to. For more on this *see* CLASSIFIERS.

about (*concerning*) guānyú [gwahn-yew]
(*approximately*) . . . zuǒyòu [dzwor-yoh]
about 4 o'clock sìdiǎn zhōng zuǒyòu [sur-dyen joong dzwor-yoh]
about the same chàbuduō yíyàng [chah-boo-dwor yee-yahng]

above (zai) . . . shàng [dzI]
Note that **shàng** comes after the word it refers to:

above the desk
zai zhuōzi shàng
[dzI jwor-dzur shahng]

accident shìgu [sher-goo]
   (*road accident*) jiāotōng shìgu [jyow-toong sher-goo]

acrobatics zájì [dzah-jee]

across (*used with verbs of motion*) guò [gwor]
   come across! guòlái! [gwor lI]
   just across the road jiùzai mǎlù duìmiànr [jyoh-dzI mah-loo dway-myenr]

acupuncture zhēnjiǔ [jun-jyoh]

ACUPUNCTURE
Acupuncture is a traditional form of Chinese medicine the origins of which go back a long way. It involves the stimulation with needles of particularly sensitive spots of the human body which are linked to the nervous system. These fine needles are inserted in the skin and vibrated either manually or by an electric current. Acupuncture is widely used to relieve pain, to act as a local anaesthetic and in therapy.

adaptor duōyòng chātóu [dwor-yoong chah-toh]

address dìzhǐ [dee-jur]
   could you write the address down? máfan nín bǎ dìzhǐ bāng wo xiě xiàlai, hǎo ma? [mah-fahn neen bah dee-jur bahng wor syeh syah-lI how mah]
   what's your address? nín zhù nǎr? [neen joo nar]

ADDRESSES
Addresses are normally written in the reverse order to that normal in the West, starting with the country and continuing with the province, town, street, number and name of the addressee. For example:

   People's Republic of China,
   Jiangxi Province,
   Jingdezhen,
   Gaoling Road, Number 7
   Zhang Jianguo

This would normally be written in Chinese characters, but Pinyin can also be used, although this is likely to slow down delivery, particularly if the street name is not written in Chinese characters. It is often difficult to work out which character a Pinyin spelling refers to and it is a good idea to get Chinese friends or colleagues to write down their addresses in characters and stick photocopies of these on envelopes. Some useful Pinyin words here are:

>**province** shěng [shung]
>**road** lù [loo]
>**number** hào [how]

ADDRESSING PEOPLE

Outside the People's Republic of China, titles roughly equivalent to Western ones are used:

>**Mr** xiānsheng [syen-shung]
>(which can also mean 'a gentleman' or 'gentlemen')

>**Mrs** fūren [foo-run]
>(also means 'a lady')

>**Miss** xiáojiě [syow-jyeh]
>(also means 'a young lady')

>**Ms** nüshì [nyew-shur]

These titles follow the surname, so, for example:

>**Mr Li**
>Lǐ xiānsheng
>[lee syen-shung]

>**Mrs Zhang**
>Zhāng fūren
>[jahng foo-run]

>**Miss Wang**
>Wáng xiáojiě
>[wahng syow-jyeh]

Western visitors to China are usually addressed by these titles, and it is quite polite for foreign visitors to use them with their Chinese hosts.

But the Chinese in the People's Republic of China do not normally address each other in the same way. Since 1949, the most common form of address has been:

>**tóngzhì** [toong-jur]

which is usually translated as 'comrade'. You can still address someone whose name you don't know as **tóngzhì** by itself. If you know their name, you can address them or refer to them as:

>**Lǐ tóngzhì**
>**Wáng tóngzhì** etc.

But this is not as universal as it once was and the word:

>**shīfu**
>[shur-foo]

which means 'master' is gaining favour as a polite way of referring to non-professional men and middle-aged women. This word also follows the surname. For example:

> **Yáng shīfu**
> [yang shur-foo]
> Master Yang

For addressing younger women it is safer to continue using **tóngzhì**. For professional people, titles often replace **tóngzhì**. So **Mr Fei** who is a head-teacher, college principal or head of a university would be referred to as:

> **Fèi xiàozhǎng**
> [fay syow-jahng]
> Principal or Headmaster Fei

And **Professor Peng** would be called:

> **Péng jiàoshòu**
> [pung jyow-show]
> Professor Peng

Mr Li, the manager of a factory, would be called:

> **Lǐ jīnglǐ**
> [lee jing-lee]
> Manager Li

Ms Zhang, who is an engineer, would be addressed as:

> **Zhāng gōngchéngshī**
> [jahng goong-chung-shur]
> Engineer Zhang

There is one attractive and typically Chinese way of referring to and addressing colleagues and friends which combines respect and affection. This is to put the words **lǎo** (old) or **xiǎo** (little or young) before the surname.

> **lǎo Wáng**
> [low wahng]

could be the manager or a colleague, and

> **xiǎo Lǐ**
> [syow lee]

might be the newest recruit to the office or a young colleague.

First names without surnames are used only between family and close friends, so foreigners are advised to avoid them unless specifically requested to use them.

Children can be addressed as:

xiǎo péngyou
[syow pung-yoh]
little friend

See also HELLO, NAMES.

ADJECTIVES

Some adjectives can come before the noun as in English, and often take the suffix **de**, especially if they are of more than one syllable. For example:

lü chá
[lyew chah]
green tea

dà hào
[dah how]
large size

yìbānde fàndiàn
[yee-bahn-der fahn-dyen]
ordinary restaurants

One special feature of the Chinese language is that adjectives used after a noun are treated as verbs, that is to say you do not use a word for 'is' or 'are' etc. with these adjectives since it is already contained in the adjective. Here are some examples of Chinese sentences which show how the equivalent of the English verb is omitted:

you are very kind
nǐ zhēn hǎo
[nee jun how]
(*literally: you very kind*)

the weather is very hot
tiānqi hěn rè
[tyen-chee hun rer]
(*literally: weather very hot*)

things are cheap here
zhèrde dōngxi piányi
[jer-der doong-syee pyen-yee]
(*literally: here things cheap*)

the hotel is not very expensive
zhèijiā fàndiàn bù hěn guì
[jay-jyah fahn-dyen boo hun gway]
(*literally: the hotel not very expensive*)

advance: in advance tíqián [tee-chyen]

ADVERBS

The commonest way of expressing an adverbial idea in Chinese is to add **de** to a verb and use the plain adjective after it. For example:

(**drive** – kāi; **quick** – kuài)

he drives very quickly
tā kāide hěn kuài

(**speak** – shuō; **clear** – qīngchu)

she speaks very clearly
tā shuōde hěn qīngchu

advertisement guǎnggào [gwahng-gow]

aeroplane fēijī [fay-jee]

after yǐhòu [yee-hoh]
after lunch chīle wǔfàn yǐhōu [chur-ler woo-fahn yee-hoh]
after you nǐ xiān qǐng [nee syen ching]

Chinese sentences can often omit the word for 'after', particularly when the completed action particle **le** is used (*see* PARTICLES). For example:

after they go we shall talk
tāmen zǒule, wǒmen zài tán
(*literally: they gone, we then talk*)

after the meal . . .
chīle fàn . . .
(*literally: eaten meal*)

afternoon xiàwǔ [syah-woo]
this afternoon jīntian xiàwǔ [jin-tyen syah-woo]
in the afternoon xiàwǔ
good afternoon ní hǎo [nee how]
(*polite form*) nín hǎo

aftershave xūhòushuǐ [syew-hoh-shway]

afterwards yǐhòu [yee-hoh]

again zài [dzI]
please say that again qǐng nǐ zài shuō yíbiàn, hǎo ma? [ching nee dzI shwor yee-byen how mah]

This **zài** is not to be confused with the word **zài** meaning 'in' or 'at', which is never stressed in a sentence.

against (*wall etc.*) kàozhe [kow-jer]

agent (*in business*) dàilǐrén [dI-lee-run]

ago yǐqián [yee-chyen]
  a year ago yìnián yǐqián [yee-nyen yee-chyen]
  two months ago liǎnge yuè yǐqián [lyahng-ger yew-eh yee-chyen]
  that was a long time ago nà shi hén jiǔ yǐqián de shì le [nah shur hun jyoh yee-chyen der shur ler]

agree: I agree wǒ tóngyì [wor toong-yee]
  do you agree? nǐ tóngyì ma? [nee toong-yee mah]
  I don't agree wǒ bù tóngyì [wor boo toong-yee]
  (*formal or business use, agreeing to do something*) **we agreed that ...** wǒmen shāngdìng ... [wor-mun shahng-ding]

agreement (*contract*) hétong [her-toong]

AGREEMENT
Chinese words cannot take different endings, so no grammatical agreement is necessary or possible.

air kōngqì [koong-chee]

air-conditioning kōngtiáo [koong-tyow]

airline hángkōng gōngsī [hahng-koong goong-sur]
  which airline is it? shi něijiā hángkōng gōngsī? [shur nay-jyah hahng-koong goong-sur]

airmail hángkōng [hahng-koong]

airmail letter hángkōng xìn [hahng-koong syin]

airport fēijīchǎng [fay-jee-chahng]   飞机场
  Beijing Capital Airport Běijīng shǒudū jīchǎng [bay-jing shoh-doo jee-chahng]
  to the airport, please qù fēijīchǎng [chyew fay-jee-chahng]

alcohol jiǔ [jyoh]
  This is the general term for alcoholic drinks. A word added in front indicates the type, for example:

  píjiǔ
  [pee-jyoh]
  beer

  pútaojiǔ
  [poo-tow-jyoh]
  wine

  Pí is a Chinese representation of the sound of the English word 'beer'.

ALCOHOL
In China you can have beer **píjiǔ** [pee-jyoh] in bottles and cans which tastes like lager (the best-

known **Qīngdǎo** [ching-dow] brand was originally produced by the Germans in Shandong province) or a cheaper brew which is served up in plastic jugs. There is wine from grapes as well as rice wine, which is similar to the Japanese **sake**. Shops in China are full of an amazing range of bottles of all shapes and sizes with a great variety of labels. These are all types of white spirit or **báijiǔ** [bI-jyoh] which are made from grain and include the (in)famous **máotái** [mow-tI] distilled from sorghum grain. These spirits are rightly called **lìhai** [lee-hI], which means 'fierce' or 'powerful'.

Although alcohol is widely available in China, it is generally consumed privately and public over-indulgence is not tolerated as it is, for example, in Japan. Nevertheless, it is quite common for visitors to be offered large quantities of alcohol at formal dinners in their honour, including a large glass of beer, a smaller one of wine and a glass of **máotái** or other spirit for toasts. Chinese hosts are quite likely to urge their guests to drink as an expression of friendliness. When toasts are drunk, the word **gānbēi** [gahn-bay], which means 'bottoms up', is an invitation to drain the glass in one go. If the guest can do this it is greatly appreciated. It is however quite acceptable to have soft drinks or **qìshuǐr** [chee-shwayr] in place of beer on these occasions.

all dōu [doh]

    we are all British wǒmen dōu shi Yīngguo ren [wor-mun doh shur ying-gwor run]

    all my money has gone wǒde qián dōu méile [wor-der chyen doh may-ler]

    that's all, thanks búyàole, xièxie [boo-yow-ler syeh-syeh]

    all right xíng [sying]

    is that all right? xíng ma?; **that's all right** xíng

almost chàbuduō [chah-boo-dwor]

    almost the same chàbuduō yíyàng [chah-boo-dwor yee-yahng]

    almost a whole day chàbuduō yì zhěngtiān [chah-boo-dwor yee jung-tyen]

If you want to say 'almost' in the sense of 'soon' or 'nearly' use the word **kuài** [kwI]:

    we're almost there
    wǒmen kuài dàole
    [wor-mun kwI dow-ler]

alone yígerén [yee-ger-run]
    I'm travelling alone wǒ yígerén lǚxíng [wor yee-ger-run lyew-sying]

ALPHABET

Chinese is written in characters, also called ideograms or ideographs, which represent meaning rather than pronunciation. But alphabets have been used for centuries by foreigners to represent the sounds of Standard Chinese and other forms of the language (*see also* DIALECTS). Most have been based on the Roman alphabet. Until the 1950s there were two main systems for representing Chinese in English: the Post Office, used for place names, and the scholarly Wade-Giles which could represent any words. 'Peking' is the Post Office form of what in Wade-Giles would be 'Pei-ching'.

In the late 1950s, the Hanyu Pinyin (or Pinyin for short) system of romanizing Standard Chinese was introduced in China, and it has become the standard both in China and internationally (but is not used in Taiwan or Hong Kong). In this system, Peking is spelt 'Beijing'. It should be stressed that these spelling changes have had no effect at all on the pronunciation of the words in China. None of these systems is universally admired, but Pinyin, as well as having official status, has the advantage of simplicity and consistency, and it is used worldwide by most newspapers, all major textbooks of spoken Standard Chinese and by most recent books about China. *See also* CHARACTERS, PINYIN.

already yǐjīng [yee-jing]

also yě [yeh]
    he's coming also tā yě lái [tah yeh lI]
    we also want to visit a factory wǒmen yé xiǎng cānguān gōngchǎng [wor-mun yeh tyahng tsahn-gwahn goong-chahng]

although suīrán [sway-rahn]

altogether yígòng [yee-goong]
    how much is that altogether? yígòng duōshǎo qián? [yee-goong dwor-show chyen]

always zǒng [dzoong]

am shì [shur]; *see* BE.

America Měiguó [may-gwor]   美国

American (*adjective*) Měiguó
(*person*) Měiguo ren
she's/he's American tā shi Měiguo ren [tah shur may-gwor run]
the Americans Měiguo ren

and gēn [gun]; hé [her]
These words are used less frequently than 'and' in English. When they are used they often mean 'with' as well as 'and'. Here are some examples:

he and I are going
wǒ gēn tā qù
[wor gun tah chyew]
(*literally: I with him go*)

Britain and China
Yīngguó gēn Zhōngguó
[ying-gwor gun joong-gwor]
(*literally: Britain with China*)

black and white
hēi bái
[hay bI]
(*literally: black white*)

They are never used to join clauses such as in:

we went into town and did some shopping
which is just:
wǒmen jìnchéng mǎile xie dōngxi
(*literally: we enter town buy (completed action particle) some things*)

another (*different*) lìngwài [ling-wI]
I'd like another room wó xiǎng lìngwài huàn ge fángjiān [wor syahng ling-wI hwahn ger fahng-jyen]
If you want to use 'another' in the sense of 'another one of the same' use the word **zài** [dzI]. For example:

another beer, please
qǐng zài lái yìbēi píjiǔ
[ching dzI lI yee-bay pee-jyoh]

I'd like another cup of coffee
wó xiǎng zài hē yìbēi kāfēi
[wor syahng dzI her yee-bay kah-fay]

answer (*noun or verb*) huídá [hway-dah]
there was no answer (*on telephone*) méi rén jiē [may run jyeh]

any rènhé [run-her]
we haven't any wǒmen méiyǒu [wor-mun may-yoh]

ANY

Note that the word **rènhé** is usually omitted in Chinese except in cases where you want to emphasize 'any'. For example:

have you any English newspapers?
nĭmen zhèr yŏu Yīngwén bàozhĭ méiyŏu?
[nee-mun jer yoh ying-wun bow-jur may-yoh]

any will do as long as it is in English
rènhé yìzhŏng dōu xíng, zhĭyào shi Yīngwénde
[run-her yee-joong doh sying jur-yow shur ying-wun-der]

anyone rènhé rén [run-her run]

did anyone come? rén láile ma? [run ll-ler mah]

is there anyone at home? jiāli yŏu rén ma? [jyah-lee yoh run mah]
See ANY.

anything rènhé shénme [run-her shun-mah]

I don't want anything wŏ shénme dōu bú yào [wor shun-mah doh boo yow]

anything else? hái yào shénme ma? [hI yow shun-mah mah]
See ANY.

APOLOGIZING

The closer you get to the ordinary Chinese in the streets, the less polite they will seem to be. They don't apologize if they bump into you. If, however, you are meeting business people then you will encounter a good deal of courtesy.

apology dàoqiàn [dow-chyen]

please accept our apologies wŏmen xiàng nín dàoqiàn [wor-mun syahng neen dow-chyen]

Another good Chinese expression for apologizing is:

wŏmen fēicháng bàoqiàn
[wor-mun fay-chahng bow-chyen]
(*literally: we feel much regret*)

approximately . . . zuŏyòu [dzwor-yoh]

April sìyue [sur-yew-eh]

are shì [shur]; *see* BE.

arm gēbo [ger-boh]

arrivals (*airport sign*) dào [dow]　进站

arrive dào [dow]
   he's arriving tomorrow tā míngtian dào [tah ming-tyen dow]

ARTICLES *see* **a, an; the**

ashtray yānhuī gāng [yen-hway gahng]

ask (*a question*) wèn [wun]
   I'll ask him wǒ wènwen tā [wor wun-wun tah]
   could you ask him? nǐ néng bù néng wènwen tā? [nee nung boo nung wun-wun tah]
   (Note the doubling of the **wèn**, which is common in everyday speech.)
   (*request*) qǐng [ching]
   he asked me to come tā qíng wǒ lái [tah ching wor lI]

asleep shuìjiào [shway-jyow]
   he's still asleep tā hái zai shuìjiào ne [tah hI dzI shway-jyow ner]

assistant zhùshǒu [joo-shoh]
   my assistant wǒde zhùshǒu [wor-der joo-shoh]

at zai [dzI]
   at my hotel zai wǒ zhù de fàndiàn [dzI wor joo der fahn-dyen]
   at the airport zai jīchǎng [dzI jee-chahng]
   at 9 o'clock jiúdiǎn zhōng [jyoh-dyen joong]

August bā-yuè [bah-yew-eh]

aunt (*father's sister*) gūgu [goo-goo]
   (*mother's sister*) yímǔ [yee-moo]

Australia Àodàlìyà [ow-dah-lee-yah]　澳大利亚

Australian (*adjective*) Àodàlìyà (de) [ow-dah-lee-yah der]
   (*person*) Àodàlìyà ren [ow-dah-lee-yah run]
   the Australians Àodàlìyà ren

autumn qiūtian [chyoh-tyen]
   in autumn qiūtian

average píngjūn [ping-jyewn]
   on average píngjūn

B

back bèi [bay]
  (*lower part*) yāo [yow]
  I've got a bad back wǒde yāo bù hǎo [wor-der yow boo how]
  I'll be right back wǒ mǎshang jiù huílai [wor mah-shahng jyoh hway-lI]
  when we go back home (*to house*) wǒmen huíjiā de shíhou [wor-mun hway-jyah der shur-hoh]
  (*to country*) wǒmen huíguó de shíhou [wor-mun hway-gwor der shur-hoh]
  back home in England we ... wǒmen Yīngguó ... [wor-mun ying-gwor ...]
  at the back zai hòumian [dzI hoh-myen]

bad bùhǎo [boo-how]
  This means literally 'not good'.

bag (*carrier-bag*) sùliao dàir [soo-lyow dIr]
  (*suitcase*) shǒutíxiāng [shoh-tee-syahng]

baggage xíngli [sying-lee]

ball-point pen yuánzhūbǐ [yew-ahn-joo-bee]

bamboo shoots sūn [soon]

bank yínháng [yin-hahng]   银行

BANK
The government-run bank, which for years was the only Chinese bank operating in China, is the People's Bank of China or **Zhōngguó Rénmín Yínháng** [joong-gwor run-min yin-hahng], which deals with Chinese currency only. Foreign currency transactions are handled by the Bank of China, or **Zhōngguó Yínháng.**

bank account zhànghù [jahng-hoo]

bank loan yínháng dàikuǎn [yin-hahng dI-kwahn]

bankrupt pòchǎn [por-chahn]

banquet yànhuì [yen-hway]

BANQUETS
Your host is likely to invite you to a banquet and you may return his hospitality at a later date. Banquets

tend to start around 6.30 and may last for two hours, beginning with small talk in an anteroom as people arrive. There will be several courses – sometimes as many as ten or even twenty – interspersed with toasts. *See* HOSPITALITY, TOASTS.

bar (*for drinks*) jiŭbājiān [jyoh-bah-jyen]

bath xĭzăo [syee-dzow]
  (*bathtub*) zăopén [dzow-pun]
  I need a bath wŏ yào xĭge zăo [wor yow syee-ger dzow]

bathroom xĭzăojiān [syee-dzow-jyen]

BATHS
Few Chinese houses have baths, although they are built into the newer flats in big cities. Some work units provide bath-houses, particularly factories where the work is dirty, and there are many public bath-houses (**yùchí**) throughout towns and cities for people who have access to neither. They are not normally open to foreigners, who would be expected to use the facilities provided in the tourist and business hotels. These are identical to those you would expect to find in the West, if a little old-fashioned in out-of-the-way places. Cleanliness is extremely important in China, but there is no ritual 'bath culture' like that found in Japan. You may well find that there is no plug in your bath or basin.

battery diànchí [dyen-chur]
Although Chinese batteries are available, they are not always that easy to find and the quality is not always very high.

be shì [shur]

BE
The verb 'to be' in Chinese is **shì**. Verbs do not take different endings for person or tense, so **shì** can mean 'am', 'is', 'are', 'was', 'were', 'will be' etc. For example:
  he is Chinese
  tā shi Zhōngguo ren
  [tah shur joong-gwor run]
  I am an engineer
  wŏ shi gōngchéngshī
  [wor shur goong-chung-shur]

they are British teachers
tāmen shi Yīngguo lǎoshī
[tah-mun shur ying-gwor low-shur]

I used to be a teacher
wǒ guòqu shi lǎoshī
[wor gwor-chyew shur low-shur]

he was my boss
tā shi wǒ lǎbǎn
[tah shur wo lah-bahn]

were they American tourists?
tāmen shi cóng Měiguo lái lǚyóu de ma?
[tah-mun shur tsoong may-gwor II lyew-yoh der mah]

Shì is never stressed in a sentence so it appears there without a tone mark.

The verb **shì** is only used when the items before it and after it are equivalent to each other, as in the sentences above. For example, in the second sentence, 'I' and 'engineer' are the same person.

There are many occasions when English uses the verb 'to be' and Chinese does not.

1. **Shì** is not often used before adjectives. For example:

this hotel is very expensive
zhèi jiā fàndiàn hěn guì
[jay jyah fahn-dyen hun gway]

Adjectives in Chinese include the idea of 'is', so in this example **guì** does not mean so much 'expensive' as 'is expensive'. *See also* ADJECTIVES.

2. To say something is 'in' or 'at' a place use the word **zài** [dzI] instead of **shì**. **Zài** means 'is in' or 'is at' and is never stressed. For example:

he is in Beijing
tā zai Běijīng
[tah dzI bay-jing]

my card is in my room
wǒde míngpiàn zai fángjiān li
[wor-der ming-pyen dzI fahng-jyen lee]

3. For 'there is' or 'there are' the word **yǒu** is used:

there is a passport on the table
zhuōzishang yǒu ge hùzhào
[jwor-dzur-shahng yoh ger hoo-jow]
(*literally: table on have passport*)

beard húzi [hoo-dzur]

Note that this word also means 'moustache' or 'whiskers'.

beautiful (*woman*) piàoliang |pyow-lyahng|
  what a beautiful day! duō hǎode tiān! |dwor how-der tyen|
  what a beautiful meal! fàn zhēn hǎo chī! |fahn jun how chur|

because yīnwei
  because he is not well yīnwei tā bu shūfu |yin-way tah boo shoo-foo|

bed chuáng |chwahng|
  I have to go to bed wó děi shùijiào le |wor day shway-jyow-ler|
  he's in bed tā shuìjiào le

bedroom wòshì |wor-shur|

BEDS
Most beds in China are of the Western variety. In rural north China many farming families sleep on a **kàng** – a raised brick or stone dais with a gap underneath for hot air from the cooking fire to pass through.

beef niúròu |nyew-roh|

beer píjiǔ |pee-jyoh|
  two beers, please lái liǎngge píjiǔ |lI lyahng-ger pee-jyoh|

BEER
Chinese beer is nearly always lager. But you can also buy a type of stout called:
  hēi píjiǔ
  |hay pee-jyoh|
which literally means 'black beer'. Most beer is bottled, but some is now canned. Different regions produce their own varieties but the most famous is **Qīngdǎo** |ching-dow| from the brewery built by German brewers in the town of Qīngdǎo.

before yǐqián |yee-chyen|
  before the next meeting wǒmen xiàci kāihuì yǐqián |wor-mun syah-tsur kI-hway yee-chyen|
  haven't we met before? zánmen yǐqián jiànguomiàn ba? |dzahn-mun yee-chyen jyen-gwor-myen bah|

begin kāishǐ |kI-shur|

behind zai . . . hòumian [dzI hoh-myen]
 the factory is behind the school gōngchǎng zai
 xuéxiào hòumian [goong-chahng dzI syew-eh-syow
 hoh-myen]
 it's behind schedule méi yǒu ànqī wánchéng [may
 yoh ahn-chee wahn-chuhng]

believe xiāngxìn [syahng-syin]
 he'll never believe it tā jué bu huì xiāngxìn [tah jyew-
 eh boo hway syahng-syin]

below (*spatially*) zai . . . xiàmian [dzI syah-myen]
 (*in amount*) zai . . . yǐxià [dzI yee-syah]

best zuìhǎo [dzway-how]
 we'll do our best wǒmen jìnlì zuò [wor-mun jin-lee
 dzwor]

better hǎo yìdiǎnr [how yee-dyenr]
 that's better hǎo duōle [how dwor-ler]

between zai . . . zhījiān [dzI . . . jur-jyen]
 between Peking and Shanghai zai Běijīng gēn
 Shànghǎi zhījiān

bicycle zìxíngchē [dzur-sying-cher]

BICYCLES

The bicycle really is as ubiquitous as it appears from
the photographs and films of China. If you check
the registration plate on the back of bicycles that you
pass, you will see that the numbers in Beijing run
into millions. Rush hour in the mornings and
evenings in the major cities is still predominantly a
bicycle rush hour interspersed with buses. The
increased number of cars and lorries is now gradually changing this and also making the problem of
traffic accidents involving bicycles even more serious. It is not uncommon to see gory photographs of
bicycle accidents and their victims in roadside
displays during safety campaigns. The Western cyc-
list should take special care and be prepared to move
out of the way of cars and buses as they will probably
not notice your bicycle.

 Bicycles can be hired in many places and there are
plenty of small independently run repair workshops
which can tackle anything from a puncture repair
upwards. The sign outside usually reads:

> **zìxíngchē xiūlǐ**
> bicycle repair shop
> [dzur-sying-cher syoh-lee]
> 自行车修理

The style of Chinese machines looks very old-fashioned to Western cyclists, as they are almost all heavy, basic, functional sit-up-and-beg cycles, designed for going to work and shopping when the ride is on level ground, rather than for long-distance touring or hill climbing. In cities it is often necessary to leave your bike in special parking places known as:

cúnchēchù
[tsoon-cher-chyew]

存车处

where they will be looked after for a few fen. No parking signs on some buildings refer to bicycles! The sign is:

cǐchù jìn fàng zixingchē!

此处禁放自行车

bid (*noun*) tóubiāo [toh-byow]

big dà [dah]

bill zhàngdānr [jahng-dahnr]
   can I have the bill, please? qǐng bāng wǒ jiězhàng, hǎo ma? [ching bahng wor jyeh-jahng how mah]

BILL

It is usual for the host to pay for formal dinners. On informal occasions the person of highest status often pays although there may be some mild argument about precedence.

bill of exchange huìpiào [hway-pyow]

birthday shēngrì [shuhng-rur]

BIRTHDAYS

Birthdays in China are not celebrated as much as in the West. The first month (**mǎnyuè**) and the first hundred days (**bǎisuì**) are celebrated for small babies with presents and special foods. Adults rarely pay much attention to their birthdays until they are sixty, when there is a great celebration. But if it is someone's birthday you can say:

zhù nǐ shēngrì kuàilè!
[joo nee shuhng-rur kI-ler]
happy birthday!

although this is rather Westernized. To an elderly person you would normally say:

> **gěi nín bàishòu**
> [gay neen bI-shoh]
> I wish you a long life

biscuit bǐnggān [bing-gahn]

bit diǎnr [dyenr]
a little bit yìdiǎnr [yee-dyenr]
a bit better hǎo yìdiǎnr [how yee-dyenr]
a bit of chocolate yìdiǎnr qiǎokelì [yee-dyenr chow-ker-lee]

black hēi [hay]

blanket tǎnzi [tahn-dzur]
(*woollen blanket*) máotǎn [mow-tahn]

bless you! (*after sneeze*)
There is no real equivalent to this in Chinese.

blood xiě [syeh]

blood group xiěxíng [syeh-sying]

blue lán [lahn]

board of directors dǒngshì huì [doong-shur hway]

boat chuán [chwahn]
by boat zuò chuán [dzwor chwahn]

body shēntǐ [shun-tee]

boiled egg zhǔ jīdàn [joo jee-dahn]

boiled rice mǐfàn [mee-fahn]
Strictly speaking this is steamed rice.

book (*noun*) shū [shoo]

border biānjìng [byen-jing]

borrow jiè [jyeh]

boss láobǎn [low-bahn]
my boss wǒde láobǎn [wor-der low-bahn]

both dōu [doh]
both of them tāmen liǎngge dōu [tah-mun lyahng-ger doh]
I'll take both zhèi liǎngge wǒ dōu yào [jay lyahng-ger wor doh yow]
Note that the word **dōu** also means 'all' in Chinese.

bottle píngzi [ping-dzur]
a bottle of beer yìpíng píjiǔ [yee-ping pee-jyoh]

bottle-opener qǐzi [chee-dzur]

bottom (*of box etc.*) dǐr [dur]

box hézi [her-dzur]

boy nánháir [nahn-hIr]

bra xiōngzhào [syoong-jow]

brake (*noun*) shāchē [shah-cher]

branch (*of company*) fēn gōngsī [fun goong-sur]

brandy báilándì [bI-lahn-dee]

breach: a breach of contract wěiyuē [way-yew-eh]

bread (*baked*) miànbāo [myen-bow]　面包
(*steamed*) mántou [mah-toh]
could I have some bread, please? lái diǎnr miànbāo,
hǎo ma? [lI dyenr myen-bow how mah]

BREAD
Although bread baked in the European style is
available in China, many northern Chinese still
prefer their bread rolls steamed in the traditional
way. This is heavy and stodgy in comparison with
Western baked bread. Bread rolls are often sold
stuffed with savoury fillings and are then known as
bāozi [bow-dzur]. In general bread is eaten most in
the wheat-growing north, southern Chinese tending
to prefer rice.

breakfast zǎofàn [dzow-fahn]

BREAKFAST
Breakfast in China is taken early, normally between
6.30 and 7.30 a.m. It is often rice gruel with pickled
vegetables, noodles or steamed bread or unsweetened doughnuts with soybean milk. Here is some useful vocabulary for this:

> **rice gruel**
> xīfàn
> [syee-fahn]
> **pickled vegetables**
> xiáncài
> [syen-tsI]
> **noodles**
> miàntiáor
> [myen-tyow-r]
> **steamed bread**
> mántou
> [mahn-toh]

unsweetened doughnuts
yóutiáo
|yoh-tyow|

soybean milk
dòujiāng
|doh-jyahng|

Breakfast will normally be eaten either at home or in one of the early opening cafés or foodstalls. Chinese breakfast is also available in the Chinese dining-rooms of hotels, although hotels used to Western visitors can supply toast, coffee and eggs at the very least and the large Joint Venture hotels in the main cities pride themselves on being able to supply quality Western cuisine.

If you should want to eat Chinese-style food at breakfast – or any other time – you just say:

I want to eat Chinese food
wó xiǎng chī Zhōngcān
|wor syahng chur joong-tsahn|

In general, the staff of hotels do not expect foreigners to want genuine Chinese food, particularly at breakfast time! So here is some vocabulary for Western breakfasts:

toast
kǎo miànbāo
|kow myen-bow|

boiled egg
zhǔ jīdàn
|joo jee-dahn|

fried egg
jiān jīdàn
|jyen jee-dahn|

scrambled eggs
chǎo jīdàn
|chow jee-dahn|

ham
huótuǐ
|hwor-tway|

milk
niúnǎi
|nyoh-nI|

bridge qiáo |chyow|
  (*card game*) qiáopái |chyow-pI|

briefcase píbāo |pee-bow|

bring dàilái [dI-lI]
  I didn't bring it with me wǒ méi dàilái [wor may dI-lI]

Britain Yīngguó [ying-gwor]　英国
  Dàbùlièdiān [dah-boo-lyeh-dyen] is the formal word for Great Britain, but **Yīngguó**, which strictly speaking means 'England' or 'English', is used for Britain and British in ordinary speech.

British Yīngguó [ying-gwor]
  I am British wǒ shi Yīngguo ren [wor shur ying-gwor run]

brochure shuōmíng shū [shwor-ming shoo]
  our company brochure wǒmen gōngsī de shuōmíng shū [wor-mun goong-sur der shwor-ming shoo]

broken (*calculator etc.*) huàile [hwI-ler]
  (*arm etc.*) duànle [dwahn-ler]

brother (*older*) gēge [ger-ger]
  (*younger*) dìdi [dee-dee]
  brothers xiōngdì [syoong-dee]

brown zōngsè [dzoong-ser]

Buddhism Fójiào [foh-jyow]

BUDDHISM

Buddhism is one of the traditional religions of China, along with Taoism and Confucianism (which is strictly speaking an ethical system rather than a religion). Like all religions, Buddhism was distrusted and discouraged by the atheist Communist Party when it came to power in 1949. It remained popular, particularly with rural people, but it was attacked during the Cultural Revolution (1966–76) as a feudal superstition and many temples and monasteries were closed down or even destroyed.

In the post-Mao era, many temples have reopened and some are training priests and nuns. New temples have also been built for the tourist trade. But the government remains ambivalent towards Buddhism. The Chinese Buddhist Association maintains ties with Buddhist communities abroad and there are showpiece monasteries like the one in the Lama Temple **Yōnghégōng** [yoong-her-goong] in northeastern Beijing. On the other hand articles appear in the press criticizing ordinary people who make offerings to Buddhist statues. If you visit temples like those in the Western or Fragrant Hills near Beijing, you will see offerings of coins, small denomination notes and sometimes fruit next to a statue or in its outstretched hand.

Buddhist (*adjective*) Fójiào(de) [foh-jyow-der]
(*noun*) Fójiào tú [foh-jyow too]

budget (*noun*) yùsuàn [yew-swahn]

building jiànzhù [jyen-joo]
(*more than one storey*) lóu [loh]

Burma Miǎndiàn [myen-dyen]

Burmese (*adjective*) Miǎndiàn(de) [myen-dyen-der]
(*noun*) Miǎndiàn ren [myen-dyen run]

bus (*within a town or city*) gōnggòng qìchē [goong-goong chee-cher]
(*long-distance bus*) chángtú qìchē [chahng-too chee-cher]
by bus zuò gònggōng qìchē [dzwor goong-goong chee-cher]

Both words are often abbreviated to:

> **qìchē**
> [chee-cher]
> vehicle

This also means 'car', but few Chinese ever travel by car – if they use **qìchē** they normally mean 'bus'.

bus station gōnggòng qìchē zǒngzhàn [goong-goong chee-cher dzoong-jahn]

bus stop gōnggòng qìchē zhàn [goong-goong chee-cher jahn]   车站

Note that this is often abbreviated to:

> **chēzhàn**
> [cher-jahn]

but this can also mean 'railway station'.

BUSES

Buses in China are incredibly cheap – quite a long journey across Beijing or one of the other major cities will cost only about 15 **fēn** (**yìmáo wǔ** [yee-mow woo]) – *see* MONEY – which is only a penny or so in English money. They are also very frequent and if you have just missed one you may well see the next one coming immediately. The disadvantage is that they are always crammed full, particularly at rush hour, and make Japanese commuter trains look almost leisurely and spacious by comparison. This is the way that most Chinese get about though (the other way is by bicycle), so if you do not try it you will never know what it feels like to be an ordinary Chinese passenger.

City maps usually show different bus routes by coloured lines and numbers and indicate bus stops and bus stations. Buses display a route plan inside, like the London Underground, but it will be in Chinese characters. Bus stops all have a name, but as this is usually written in characters only, you will have to learn the correct pronunciation for your stop and hope that the overworked conductor or a helpful passenger will tap you on the shoulder when you get there. The conductors sit in special seats and you may have to fight your way through to buy a ticket. If you fail to do this you are likely to be shouted at as bus staff are under pressure to stop fare-avoidance.

Here are some useful phrases:

please tell me when we get to ...
dào ..., qǐng gàosu wǒ yixià, hä ma?
[dow ... ching gow-soo wor yee-syah how mah]

is this the right stop for ...?
zhèi zhàn shi ... ma?
[jay jahn shur ... mah]

could you write it down?
qǐng nín géi wo xiěxiàlai, hǎo ma?
[ching neen gay wor sye-syah-ll how mah]

business (*company*) gōngsī [goong-sur]
(*trade*) shēngyi [shuhng-yee]
I'm here on business wǒ lái zhèr zuò shēngyi [wor ll jer dzwor shuhng-yee]

it's a pleasure to do business with you gēn nín yìqǐ zuò shēngyi fēicháng gǎoxìng [gun neen yee-chee dzwor shuhng-yee fay-chahng gow-sying]
we look forward to a fruitful business relationship xīwàng wǒmen néng háohǎo hézuò [syee-wahng wor-mun nuhng how-how her-dzwor]
business is business gōngshìr shi gōngshìr [goong-shur shur goong-shur]
There is also a phrase:

wó yǒu shìr
[wor yoh shur]

which literally means:

I have some business to do
but which is used as a polite way of getting away from somebody.

BUSINESS

Before the current reform programme began in 1978, relatively few foreign firms did business with China and those that did had to contend with a great deal of suspicion, misunderstanding and bureaucratic obstruction. As part of the modernization campaign, the insistence on central control over all aspects of the economy has been relaxed and individual local authorities and companies are now finding it easier to do business directly with Western firms.

Until 1949 China was one of the most mercantile countries in the world and this has never been completely forgotten. However, the concepts and language of business were alien to those brought up in the puritanical Maoist days of the Cultural Revolution in the 1960s and 1970s. Many of these people are now in their late thirties and early forties and working in senior managerial or technical positions. As a generation, they have taken to Western business methods with enormous enthusiasm and there is now a vogue for Western-style business journals and books on topics like systems analysis. Links with business schools in the West are sought.

Because China is such a huge and diverse country, it is difficult to generalize about the way business should be conducted. Dealing with a small firm or county council in rural China will be very different from negotiating with a large organization in forward-looking cities like Shanghai or Guangzhou (Canton) which have longer traditions of dealing with foreigners, or in one of the Special Economic Zones near Hong Kong and Fuzhou which were specifically established to attract foreign investment. Many initial contacts take place at trade fairs, either the major ones like the Export Commodity Fairs held in the spring and autumn in Guangzhou or fairs and exhibitions organized by particular industries.

Rapidly changing economic conditions and the modernization of legal and commercial practice make it very difficult for Western businessmen to keep up to date with the latest developments. Business schools, universities, and organizations like the Sino-British Trade Council hold seminars from time to time and *China Daily*, which is published in English, carries economic and business news every day and has a special business supplement on Mondays.

In general, it seems to take a considerable time to establish business relationships with Chinese organizations. Traditional attitudes towards proper relationships combined with an element of mistrust of foreigners, which goes back at least to the Opium Wars of the early nineteenth century, make it essential for foreign companies to take their time establishing friendly and respectful relationships rather than trying to push a deal through. Foreign companies who have slowly established a relationship of mutual confidence with a Chinese counterpart have found their initial patience repaid in the long run. At a time when businessmen from all over Europe, the U S A and Japan are struggling to enter the China market, there can also be a feeling that the Chinese are setting the different nationalities against each other – playing off the barbarians, is a traditional Chinese phrase.

The initial contacts between Chinese and Western businessmen are likely to consist of meetings where tea and small talk seem to dominate and business is hardly mentioned. Host organizations are certain to entertain their guests to a banquet and reciprocal hospitality, particularly in prolonged negotiations, is an indication that a firm is intending to conform to the Chinese way of doing things. Business cards are now used by Chinese businessmen, and also by government and party officials and academics. It is a wise move to have your card printed with a Chinese translation of your name, status in the company and company name on the back.

business card míngpiàn |ming-pyen|

business trip chūchāi |choo-chI|

businessman shāngrén |shahng-run|

businesswoman shāngrén |shahng-run|

busy (*person*) máng |mahng|
   I'm busy wǒ hěn máng |wor hun mahng|
   the line is busy zhànxiàn |jahn-syen|
   it's a busy road zhèi tiáo lù chē hěn duō |jay tyow loo cher hun dwor|
   it's a busy place zhèr hěn rènao |jer hun rer-now|

but kěshi |ker-shur|
   I went to the hotel but he wasn't there wǒ qùguo

fàndiàn, kěshi tā búzài [wor chyew-gwor fahn-dyen ker-shur tah boo-dzI]

Note that you do not always need a word for 'but' in a Chinese sentence, for example:

> **not in London but over here** (*in China*)
> búzài Lúndūn, zài (Zhōngguó) zhèr
> (*literally: not in London, (in China) here*)

butter huángyóu [hwahng-yoh]
Butter is not part of Chinese cuisine but you can get it in hotels. Tibetans put butter from yak milk in their tea.

button niǔkòu [nyew-koh]

buy mǎi [mI]
Do not confuse this word with **mài**, which means 'to sell'!

by: by train zuò huǒchē [dzwor hwor-cher]
by plane zuò fēijī [dzwor fay-jee]
by bicycle qí zìxíngchē [chee dzur-sying-cher]
it's made by ... shì ... zhìzàode [shur ... jur-dzow-der]
we'll have to know by ... wǒmen ... yǐqián bìxu zhīdao [wor-mun ... yee-chyen bee-syew jur-dow]

C

café kāfēi diàn [kah-fay dyen]

CAFÉS

There are few cafés in the Western sense apart from café-type bars in the modern hotels. In some tourist areas, enterprising people have opened cafés catering for Western tastes. The privately owned **Wenyuan** [wen-yew-ahn] café on **Xidan** [syee-dahn], one of Beijing's major shopping streets, is open till 11 p.m. – which is very late for China – and serves cold drinks, snacks including Western food and coffee. But Chinese are more likely to take their refreshment in a teahouse or a restaurant or from wayside stalls serving tea and snacks. Parks and cultural sites usually have refreshment stalls serving tea, soft drinks and light snacks. At Beihai Park in Beijing, for example, you can sip tea or eat a plate of mostly meaty mixed cold dishes (**lěng pīnpánr**) [lung pin-pahnr] in a pavilion by the side of the boating lake. *See also* TEA.

cake dàngāo [dahn-gow]

calculator jìsuànqì [jee-swahn-chee]

Do not confuse this with the word **jìsuànjī**, which means 'computer'.

CALENDAR

Each year of the traditional Chinese calendar, which lasts twelve or thirteen lunar months and begins in January or February by the Western calendar, was thought to be under the influence of one of twelve animals. The animal of the year of a person's birth supposedly influences that person's character.

Here is a list of the twelve animals and the years which they represent:

1936	1948	1960	1972	1984	**rat** shǔ [shoo]
1937	1949	1961	1973	1985	**ox** niú [nyoh]
1938	1950	1962	1974	1986	**tiger** hǔ [hoo]
1939	1951	1963	1975	1987	**hare** tù [too]
1940	1952	1964	1976	1988	**dragon** lóng [loong]
1941	1953	1965	1977	1989	**snake** shé [sher]
1942	1954	1966	1978	1990	**horse** mǎ [mah]
1943	1955	1967	1979	1991	**goat** yáng [yahng]

1944	1956	1968	1980	1992	**monkey** hóu [hoh]
1945	1957	1969	1981	1993	**cock** jī [jee]
1946	1958	1970	1982	1994	**dog** gŏu [goh]
1947	1959	1971	1983	1995	**boar** zhū [jyew]

You can use the twelve-year cycle as an indirect way of asking somebody's age. For example:

ní shŭ shénme de?
[nee shoo shun-mah der]
which (animal) do you belong to?

wó shŭ zhū
[wor shoo jyew]
I belong to boar

Remember that if your birthday is in January or February you may belong to the previous year by the Chinese calendar.

call: what's it called? zhèige jiào shénme? [jay-ger jyow shun-mah]
I'd like to make an international long-distance call to London wŏ yàoge guójì chángtú, dào Lúndūn de [wor yow-ger gwor-jee chahng-too dow loon-doon der]
I'll call back later (*on phone*) wŏ guò yīhuìr zài dă [wor gwor yee-hway-r dzI dak]

camera zhàoxiàngjī [jow-syang-jee]

can: can I ...? wŏ néng ... ma? [wor nung ...mah]
I can't ... wŏ bù néng ... [wor boo nung]
can you ... ? nĭ néng ... ma?
you can't ... nĭ bù néng ...
he can't ... tā bù néng ...
can we ... ? wŏmen néng ... ma?
we can't ... wŏmen bù néng ...
can they ... ? tāmen néng ... ma?
they can't ... tāmen bù néng ...

CAN

Another word that can be used interchangeably with **néng** as given above is **kéyĭ** [ker-yee].

The word **huì** [hway] is often used where something has been learned:

he can speak Chinese
tā huì jiăng Hànyŭ
[tah hway jyahng hahn-yew]

Canada Jiānádà [jyah-nah-dah]　加拿大

cancel tuì [tway]
   can I cancel it? néng/kěyi tuì ma? [ker-yee tway mah]

Cantonese (*adjective*) Guǎngdōng [gwahng-doong]
   (*person*) Guǎngdōng ren [gwahng-doong run]
   (*language*) Guǎngdōng huà

capital (*money*) zīběn [dzur-bun]
   (*for small businesses*) běnqián [bun-chyen]

capital city shǒudū [shoh-doo]

car (xiǎo) qìchē [(syow) chee-cher]
   by car zuò qìchē [dzwor chee-cher]
   Most cars in China are taxis or are owned and run by
   government organizations. A growing number of
   wealthy individuals have their own cars but they are
   a tiny minority and are likely to remain so.

car hire qìchē chūzū [chee-cher choo-dzoo]
   Note that in China 'car hire' means hiring a car plus
   driver, self-drive car hire not being available yet.

car park tíngchē chǎng [ting-cher chahng]
   In practice this usually means a coach and taxi park
   near a tourist site.

card (*business*) míngpiàn [ming-pyen]

care of qíng zhuǎnjiāo . . . [jwahn-jyow]

carpet dìtǎn [dee-tahn]

case (*suitcase*) shǒutíxiāng [shoh-tee syahng]

cash (*money*) xiàn qián [syen chyen]
   can you cash this cheque for me? nǐ néng duìhuàn
   yíxia zhèizhāng zhīpiào ma? [nee nung dway-hwahn
   yee-syah jay-jahng jur-pyow mah]

cassette héshì cídài [her-shur tsur-dI]

cassette recorder héshì lùyīnjī [her-shur loo-yin-jee]

catch: I'll catch the next train wó gǎn xiàtàng huǒchē
   qù [wor gahn syah-tahng hwor-cher chyew]
   where do I catch a bus for . . .? qù . . . zai nǎr zuò
   chē? [chyew . . . dzI nar dzwor cher]

central heating nuǎnqì [nwahn-chee]

centre zhōngxīn [joong-syin]

chair yǐzi [yee-dzur]

chairman (*of company*) dǒngshi zhǎng [doong-shur
   jahng]
   (*of country*) zhǔxí [jyew-syee]
   Chairman Mao Máo zhǔxí [mow jyew-syee]

change: can I change some money? wǒ kéyǐ huàn diǎnr
qián ma? [wor ker-yee hwahn dyenr chyen mah]
   could you give me some small change for this? nín
néng géi wo diǎnr líng de ma? [neen nung gay wor
dyenr ling der mah]
   do I have to change trains? yào huàn chē ma? [yow
hwahn cher mah]
   I'd like to change my flight wó xiǎng huàn yíxia fēijī
[wor syahng hwahn yee-syah fay-jee]
   (*noun*) **we've made some changes to the design**
zhèige shèji wǒmen gǎile yíxia [jay-ger sher-jee, wor-
mun gI-ler yee-syah]

CHARACTERS

Chinese, uniquely among the world's languages, is
written without any alphabet. The writing – which is
known in Chinese as **Hànzì** [hahn-dzur] – has been
called ideographic or pictographic as some characters originally evolved from pictorial represen-
tations of things or ideas. The following examples
illustrate this evolution:

sun	0	θ	日
moon	𝔻	𝓎	月
water	𝔦	𝔦	水
sheep	𝔊	𝔜	羊
fire	𝔴	𝔴	火

Each character is made up of a number of brush or
pen strokes. One stroke only or as many as twenty
may be needed to draw a character. For example:

one	一
toad	蟾

Each stroke has to be made in the right direction,
and there is a correct order for writing the strokes of

each character. In everyday writing, ballpoints or fountain pens are used. The Chinese writing brush (**máobǐ** [mow-bee]) is used today only for traditional calligraphy, which is still highly valued as an art form.

Characters may also be combined in various ways to give new meanings. For example:

wood 木

forest 林

Many present-day characters are made up of two parts, one indicating the meaning and the other the sound, for example:

mother mā 妈

female (meaning) 女

mǎ (sound) 马

father bà 爸

father (meaning) 父

bā (sound) 巴

There may be as many as 60,000 characters in existence but many are obsolete or obscure. A highly literate Chinese would probably need to be able to recognize about 6,000 to 8,000 characters, although he or she may not always remember some of the less frequent ones. For everyday reading a knowledge of 3,000 characters is normally considered to be adequate.

The large number of characters that has to be memorized has led to serious illiteracy. The present government began a series of reforms in the 1950s to simplify the characters by reducing the number of strokes in some of them so as to make the language easier to read and write. The characters used in the People's Republic are simplified characters, **jiántǐzì**, but all Taiwanese and most Hong Kong publications retain the older and more complex full-form characters or **fántǐzì**.

For example, the word for China – **Zhōngguó** – is written:

中国

in simplified characters and:

中國

in the full form.

Written Chinese had an influence on East Asia comparable to that of Latin in Europe. Japanese, Korean and Vietnamese were first written in Chinese characters. Japanese still uses about 2,000 Chinese characters, known as **kanji** (the Japanese pronunciation of **Hànzì**), and Korean in South Korea also uses them although they were phased out in Vietnam many years ago.

cheap piányi [pyen-yee]
it's cheap hǎo piányi [how pyen-yee]

check: I'll check it wó jiǎnchá yíxia [wor jyen-chah yee-syah]
could you please check that? qíng ni jiǎnchá jiǎnchá, hǎo ma? [ching nee jyen-chah jyen-chah how mah]

cheerio zàijiàn [dzI-jyen]

cheers (*toast*) gānbēi [gahn-bay]

cheese nǎilào [nI-low]
Cheese is unknown in the diet of the Han Chinese, who tend to shun dairy products. Mongols and other minority groups eat products similar to cream cheese.

chemist's yàofáng [yow-fahng] 药房

cheque zhīpiào [jur-pyow]
can I pay by cheque? kāi zhīpiào, xíng ma? [kI jur-pyow sying mah]

cheque-book zhīpiào bù [jur-pyow boo]

cheque card zhīpiào kǎ [jur-pyow-kah]
These are not yet widely used or understood in China.

CHEQUES

China's banking and finance system has been in constant flux during the modernization drive of the 1980s and information is likely to become out of date very quickly. You can cash *traveller's* cheques at the large hotels, tourist shops and branches of the Bank of China with no difficulty. *Personal* cheques can sometimes be cashed by foreigners at the Bank of China in some cities when backed by some of the internationally known credit cards, but this may be risky. It is advisable to check with local branches of the Bank of China in Britain or with travel agents to find out current regulations. *See also* CREDIT CARDS.

chest (*of body*) xiōng [syoong]

chicken jī [jee]

child háizi [hI-dzur]

children háizi [hI-dzur]

CHILDREN

The Chinese are very fond of small children and they are usually indulged and fussed over. As the one-child family is the official norm, there are now worries about the effects of having a generation of spoilt 'little emperors'. It is rare to see children behaving badly in public and they approach foreigners with a mixture of fascination and suspicion. Toddlers barely able to talk are likely to point at you and say loudly:

> **wàiguo ren**
> [wI-gwor run]
> foreigner

If you are talking to a child you can address him or her as:

> **xiǎo péngyou**
> [syow pung-yoh]
> little friend

China Zhōngguó [joong-gwor] 中国

Literally the word for China means 'the middle kingdom'. China (the People's Republic of China or **Zhōnghuá Rénmín Gònghéguó**) is not to be confused with the Republic of China (**Zhōnghuá Mínguó**), which is Taiwan. China views Taiwan as a breakaway part of the motherland which will eventually be re-integrated. Only the People's Republic of China is represented in the United Nations.

Chinese (*adjective*) Zhōngguó [joong-gwor]
(*person*) Zhōngguo ren [joong-gwor run]
(*language*) Zhōngwén, Hànyǔ [joong-wun, hahn-yew]
the Chinese Zhōngguo rémín [joong-gwor run-min]
Of the two words given for the Chinese language the first tends to mean the written language.
See DIALECTS.

Chinese tea Zhōngguo chá [joong-gwor chah]

chips zhá tǔdòu tiáo [jah too-doh tyow]
Chips won't be found in China outside the Western-style restaurants of the more expensive hotels.

chocolate qiāokelì [chow-ker-lee]

chopsticks kuàizi [kwI-dzur]

CHOPSTICKS
In general there is no special etiquette for using chopsticks. In families and at ordinary meals most people will use any chopsticks they are given, although some fastidious individuals do insist on having their own. At formal meals and banquets and in the restaurants of the top hotels you will probably be supplied with new chopsticks in a long paper envelope which may well have the name of the establishment printed on it. At formal meals chopsticks may be rested on special enamel chopstick rests, but normally they are just placed on the bowl or side plate. Again, at banquets, there is sometimes a longer pair of chopsticks for the host to use to serve the guest of honour. *See also* EATING HABITS.

Christian name míngzi [ming-dzur]

CHRISTIAN NAMES
For Chinese the term 'Christian name' is inappropriate and best avoided. The Chinese given name (not first name since it follows the surname) generally consists of one or two syllables. Zhōu Ēnlái's given name, therefore, was Ēnlái and Máo Zédōng's was Zédōng. It is not polite to use someone's given name without the surname unless you know them really well. *See also* ADDRESSING PEOPLE, NAMES.

CHRISTIANITY

Christianity is a minority religion mostly confined to the large cities and areas where European missionaries operated in the late nineteenth and early twentieth centuries. Chinese Christians have had a difficult time since 1949. The Catholic Church had to break away from Rome in the 1950s and still retains the Latin mass. Protestant groups were all combined into one church. Catholicism (**tiānzhǔjiào**) and Protestantism (**jīdūjiào**) are thought of as separate religions.

Christmas shèngdàn jié [shung-dahn jyeh]

CHRISTMAS

Christmas in China is celebrated only by Chinese Christians and the expatriate foreign community and is not really significant for most Chinese. *See* NEW YEAR.

church jiàotáng [jyow-tahng]

CHURCHES

During the Cultural Revolution of the 1960s and 70s many churches were destroyed or converted to secular use. The same fate befell Buddhist temples and monasteries. Some have now reopened and there are functioning cathedrals in Beijing and Shanghai. You can also come across tiny churches in the countryside.

cigar xuějiā [syew-eh-jyah]

cigarette xiāngyān [syahng-yen]

cine-camera diànyǐng shèyǐngjī [dyen-ying shur-ying-jee]

cinema diànyǐng yuàn [dyen-ying yew-ahn]

city chéngshi [chung-shur]

city centre shì zhōngxīn [shur joong-syin]

class *see* FIRST CLASS.

CLASSIFIERS

Classifiers in Chinese are special words that are used when you want to combine a number word with a noun – when, for example, you want to say: three books, six people or fifteen postcards etc.

In English there is something similar to this in the usages: two *cups of* tea, three *bunches of* flowers, six *head of* cattle. The difference is that in English you do not always need these 'classifiers': in Chinese you do.

There are a great many different classifiers in Chinese (a recent textbook has listed seventy-eight!) and each noun should take the appropriate one depending on what 'class' of object it belongs to. Here is a list of the most important and common classifiers:

bēi	[bay]	cups or glasses of something
běn	[bun]	books and magazines
dùn	[doon]	meals
duŏ	[dwoh]	flowers, clouds
fèn	[fun]	newspapers
fēng	[fung]	letters and telegrams
hé	[her]	boxes of something
jiā	[jyah]	restaurants, hotels and shops
jiān	[jyen]	rooms
jiàn	[jyen]	pieces of work, items of clothing
kuàir	[kwIr]	lumps of food, coal, soap
liàng	[lyahng]	vehicles
píng	[ping]	bottles of something
shuāng	[shwahng]	pairs of things
tiáo	[tyow]	rivers, roads, fish, dogs, legs, skirts and trousers
wèi	[way]	people, when being respectful, so especially with teachers and guests
zhāng	[jahng]	tables, beds, maps, sheets of paper
zhī	[jur]	hands, feet, cats, sheep, birds, chicken
zuò	[dzwor]	mountains, bridges, pagodas, large buildings, statues

The usual word order when using a classifier is:
  number + classifier + noun
So:

  yì běn shū
  [yee bun shoo]
  one book

liǎng zhāng dìtú
[lyahng jahng dee-too]
two maps

sān píng qìshuǐ
[sahn ping chee-shway]
three bottles of fizzy pop

sì fēng xìn
[sur fung syin]
four letters

wǔ tiáo yú
[woo tyow yew]
five fish

liù liàng qìchē
[lyoh lyahng chee-cher]
six cars

qī wèi lǎoshī
[chee way low-shur]
seven teachers

bā zuò shān
[bah dzwor shahn]
eight mountains

jiǔ jiān wūzi
[jyoh jyen woo-dzur]
nine rooms

shí kuàir qiǎokelì
[shur kwIr chow-ker-lee]
ten pieces of chocolate

The most common classifier of all is a general one:

gè
[ger]

which can go with a whole range of things, including people when you do not need to be especially polite in referring to them:

wǔ ge Yīngguo ren
[woo ger ying-gwor run]
five English people

Gè is never stressed in sentences, so it appears without a tone mark. In colloquial speech the classifier **gè** is being used more and more to replace the official classifiers. People might, therefore, say:

yí ge yóupiao
[yee ger yoh-pyow]
a stamp

instead of:

>**yì zhāng yóupiao**
>a stamp

or: **liǎng ge bǐ**
>[lyahng ger bee]
>two pens

instead of:

>**liǎng zhī bǐ**
>two pens

There are some apparent exceptions to the rule that you need a classifier after a number.

The words **nián** for 'year' and **tiān** for 'day' are considered to be classifiers in their own right and do not need an additional one. So you say:

>**sān tiān**
>[sahn tyen]
>three days

>**wǔ nián**
>[woo nyen]
>five years

Months take the classifier **gè**. So:

>**sān ge yuè**
>[sahn ger yew-eh]
>three months

This is to distinguish it from **sān yuè**, which means 'March' – *see also* DATES.

Classifiers must also be used after the words for 'this' and 'that' – **zhèi** and **nèi**:

>**that book**
>nèi běn shū
>[nay bun shoo]

>**this hotel**
>zhèi jiā fàndiàn
>[jay dzwor fahn-dyen]

There is a special classifier **xiē**, which converts **nèi** and **zhèi** into the plurals 'those' and 'these'. It then replaces any other classsifier:

>**those books**
>nèi xiē shū
>[nay syeh shoo]

>**these hotels**
>zhèi xiē fàndiàn
>[jay syeh fahn-dyen]

clean (*adjective*) gānjing [gahn-jing]

clock zhōng [joong]

closed guānle [gwahn-ler]

clothes yīfu [yee-foo]

CLOTHES

Everyday dress in China tends to be casual but discreet. The conformist days of the 1960s and 70s when only blue, green and grey coats and trousers were really acceptable have now gone. Greater prosperity and a more open-minded attitude have led to a greater range of colours, but styles are often limited.

Summer wear for men tends to be a white shirt and light, loose trousers although T-shirts, jeans and track suits are popular with teenagers. Older women still favour trousers, but younger ones now appear in summer dresses or skirts and blouses.

Winter clothing, particularly in the north, disguises the sexes as everyone wraps up in padded jackets and fur hats with earflaps to avoid freezing.

For special occasions, Chinese may wear either a more formal version of their casual clothes or, increasingly, Western suits. The once universal high-collared jacket known in the West as the Mao jacket is still seen. This is known as a

zhōngshānzhuāng
[joong-shahn-jwahng]

being named after Sun Yatsen (Sūn Zhōngshān), the inspiration of China's nationalist revolution at the beginning of this century.

Traditional formal wear for women is the long and elegant

qípáo
[chee-pow]

which is a high-necked dress with a slit from the hem to the knee. This is being worn increasingly by female staff in hotels and clubs.

Foreign visitors can comfortably wear suits to meetings but casual dress should be more restrained than in the West, particularly for women – shorts and low-cut dresses or blouses tend to be frowned on, although youthful foreign backpackers dressed like this are becoming more common.

coat (*overcoat*) dàyī [dah-yee]

code (*dialling*) cháng tú qūhào [chahng too chyew-how]

coffee kāfēi [kah-fay]
 black coffee bù jiā nǎide kāfēi [boo jyah nI-der kah-fay]
 white coffee jiā nǎide kāfēi

COFFEE

Coffee is not a very common drink in China. You are far more likely to be offered tea or even just boiled water. Larger hotels and some of the more enterprising new cafés catering for tourists will, however, be able to serve you a fairly expensive cup of imported coffee. In restaurants tea is the usual accompaniment to a meal.

coin yìngbì [ying-bee]
 See MONEY.

cold lěng [lung]
 it's cold (*weather*) tiānqi hén lěng [tyen-chee hun lung]
 I've got a cold wó gǎnmào le [wor gahn-mow ler]

colour yánsè [yen-ser]

colour film cǎisè jiāojuǎnr [tsI-ser jyow-jyew-ahnr]

comb (*noun*) shūzi [shoo-dzur]

come lái [lI]
 he's coming tomorrow tā míngtian lái [tah-ming-tyen lI]
 I come from . . . wǒ shi . . . ren [wor shur . . . run]
 when are you coming to England? nǐ shénme shíhou lái Yīngguó? [nee shun-mah shur-hoh lI ying-gwor]

committed: we are committed to this zhèige wǒmen yídìng yào zuò [jay-ger wor-mun yee-ding yow dzwor]

Communism gòngchán zhǔyì [goong-chahn joo-yee]

COMMUNISM

China has been governed by the Communist Party since 1949 and although the 1980s have seen far greater flexibility and openness than at any time since 1949, the government still insists that China is to remain basically a socialist society.

Communist Party Gòngchándǎng [goong-chahn-dahng]

COMMUNIST PARTY

There are perhaps 40 million members of the Chinese Communist Party and it is the single most powerful force in China, not only in central government but in all walks of life. Every organization has its own management structure, but in addition most have a Party Committee which wields a great deal of power. In years gone by, the Party Committee would have the final, and sometimes the only, say in major decisions. Since the current modernization programme began, the influence of the Party has been reduced, and technical, economic and management specialists can play more of a role in decision-making. However, Party diehards are not willing to surrender all their power and influence. It is usually very difficult to distinguish who are the important Party members in any organization. In a school or college you may even find that the headmaster or professor is not a Party member but that one of the cleaning staff is. The Thirteenth Party Congress of October 1987 decided to reduce Party control but it will be some time before the effect of this is clear.

company (*business*) gōngsī [goong-sur]

COMPARISON

With its typical economy of utterance and disdain for stating more than the context requires Chinese does not normally or necessarily distinguish between words like 'good/better', 'big/bigger' etc. unless a specific comparison is being made. So, for example:

> **zhèige hǎo**

could mean either:

> this is good

or: this is better

depending on the context. If you think about it, saying 'this is good' is perfectly adequate as an expression of approval.

Similarly:

> **nèige dà**

could mean either:

> that is big

or: that is bigger

depending on context.

But you can use the words:

> **diǎnr** or **yìdiǎnr**
> [dyenr, yee-dyenr]

a bit
de duō
[der dwor]
much

to express the degree of a comparison, for example:

it's a lot bigger/better
dà/hǎo de duō

it's a bit bigger/better
dà/hǎo diǎnr

If, however, a specific comparison is being made, then you use the word **bǐ** which means 'compared with'. To say **A is bigger than B**, what you say in Chinese is:

A bǐ B dà
(*literally: A compared with B big*)

China is bigger than England
Zhōngguo bǐ Yīngguo dà

To say that something is not as big, you use **méiyou** – hasn't:

England is not as big as China
Yīngguo méiyou Zhōngguo dà
(*literally: England has not got China's bigness*)

Forming the superlative is equally simple. You just put the word **zuì** [dzway] (most) in front of the adjective:

big	dà
biggest	zuì dà
good	hǎo
best	zuì hǎo
cold	lěng
coldest	zuì lěng
hot	rè
hottest	zuì rè

competitive jìngzhēng [jing-jung]
  competitive prices jìngzhēng jiàgé [jing-jung jyah-ger]

complaint bàoyuàn [bow-yew-ahn]

computer jìsuànjī [jee-swahn-jee]
  The word **diànnǎo** [dyen-now] which means 'electronic brain' is also used colloquially.

conditions (*of contract*) tiáojiàn [tyow-jyen]

conference huìyì, dàhuì [hway-yee, dah-hway]

conference room (*in hotel etc.*) huìyìshì [hway-yee-shur]

CONNECTIONS

Chinese people build up a network of connections or **guānxi** [gwahn-syee] through family ties, education and work, and these connections are extremely important when they want to get anything done. The official system is often cumbersome and over-bureaucratic, and if you can 'pull' your connections or **lā guānxi** in a particular organization, the procedure is likely to be smoother. Westerners also acquire **guānxi** when they are in regular contact with China and they may eventually become old friends or **lǎo péngyou** to the businesses or departments they deal with (*see* FRIENDS). This means in effect that they get preferential treatment as the organization does not have to go through all the tedious preliminaries of establishing credentials.

consignment (*of goods*) yì pī [yee pee]

constipation biànbì [byen-bee]

consul lǐngshì [ling-shur]
   the British consul Yīngguó lǐngshì [ying-gwor ling-shur]

contact liánxi [lyen-syee]
   I'll get in contact with him wǒ gēn tā liánxi yíxianr [wor gun tah lyen-syee yee-syenr]
   where can I contact you? wǒ dào nǎr zháo nǐ liánxi? [wor dow nar jow nee lyen-syee?]

contact lenses wúxíng yǎnjìng [woo-sying yen-jing]

container (*for shipping*) jízhuāng xiāng [jee-jwahng syahng]

contract (*noun*) hétong [her-toong]

cool (*weather*) liángkuai [lyahng-kwI]

corkscrew jiǔ qǐzi [jyoh chee-dzur]

corner jiǎor [jyow-r]
   in the corner (*of room*) wūjiǎor [woo-jyow-r]
   at the street corner jiējiǎor [jyeh-jyow-r]

correct (*adjective*) duì [dway]
   that's correct duì

Note that Chinese sometimes uses this word **duì** to mean yes (*see* YES).

cost (*noun*) jiàqián [jyah-chyen]
   let's look at the costs wǒmen xiān kànkan jiàqián [wor-mun syen kahn-kahn jyah-chyen]
   the cost of . . . . . . de jiàqián

what does it cost? duōshăo qián? [dwor-show chyen]

cotton wool yàomián [yow-myen]

could: could I ...? wŏ kéyĭ ... ma? [wor ker-yee ... mah]
could you ...? nín kéyĭ ... ma? [neen ker-yee ... mah]
See also CAN.

country (*nation*) guójiā [gwor-jyah]

couple: a couple of ... liăng ge ... [lyahng-ger]

course: of course! dāngrán! [dahng-rahn]

crazy shénjīngbìng [shung-jing-bing]
that's crazy! shénjīngbìng!

cream (*on food, for coffee*) năiyóu [nI-yoh]
(*for face*) cāliänyóu [kah-lyahn-yoh]

credit card xìnyòng kă [syin-yoong kah]
I've lost my credit cards wŏ de xìnyòng kă diūle [wor der syin-yoong kah dyoh-ler]

CREDIT CARDS

The large Joint Venture hotels, banks and Friendship Stores in large cities are used to handling the major international credit cards, but you should not expect to be able to use them in ordinary shops and restaurants. The Bank of China issued its own Great Wall Card in 1987 but this is probably of use mainly to long-term residents.

crisis wēijī [way-jee]

crowd rénqún [run-chyewn]

crowded yōngjĭ [yoong-jee]

cultural exchange wénhuà jiāoliú [wun-hwah jyow-lyoh]

Cultural Revolution wénhuà dà gémìng [wun-hwah dah ger-ming]

CULTURAL REVOLUTION

In any discussion in China about political or economic developments someone is bound to say that things have been different since the Cultural Revolution or that it would not have been possible to do something during or before the Cultural Revolution. The Cultural Revolution was a watershed in Chinese development and it is essential to understand what it was about if the current drive towards modernization and Westernization is to make any sense at all.

The Cultural Revolution was launched in the summer of 1966 by Máo Zédōng, who by then had been Chairman of the Chinese Communist Party for thirty-one years and who had been an effective ruler of China for seventeen of them. The reasons given for the campaign that was unleashed were that Chinese culture was becoming bourgeois and had to be made more proletarian. Political argument in conferences and in the press soon gave way to demonstrations when Mao sanctioned mass action against his opponents inside the Communist Party. Within months China was in turmoil. Students and factory workers organized themselves into political factions, sometimes armed, and violence spread throughout the country. The economy was disrupted and unrest became so serious that the army had to be brought in to govern many areas. Order was eventually restored, but the political paranoia that the Cultural Revolution left behind created a condition of inertia in which people dared not act for fear of being denounced. This state of affairs did not really come to an end until Mao Zedong died in 1976 and his wife and her associates – the Gang of Four or **sìren bāng** [sur-run bahng] who were blamed for many of the excesses of the Cultural Revolution – were brought to trial.

One of the most important outcomes of the Cultural Revolution – although not one its architects would have intended – is the deep distrust of ideology and revolutionary rhetoric that it has left behind. Western ideas and methods are proving extremely attractive to Chinese who have lost confidence in the Marxist-Leninist values of the 1960s and 1970s.

cup bēi [bay]
    a cup of tea yìbēi chá [yee-bay chah]

cushion diànzi [dyen-dzur]

custom fēngsu xíguàn [fung-soo syee-gwahn]
    a Chinese custom Zhōngguo de fēngsu xíguàn [joong-gwor der fung-soo syee-gwahn]

CUSTOM
Chinese attitudes to traditional customs such as festivals and fairs, folk religion and ancestor worship have veered from repression to toleration over the

last thirty or forty years. Traditional beliefs and customs have not died out but Chinese people are very discreet about how they practise them. The present tolerant climate has seen a revival of popular Buddhism and old-fashioned wedding ceremonies, particularly in the countryside. People have learned to tread carefully, knowing that a political campaign could be launched at any time attacking traditions as 'feudal superstitions'.

customer (*of company*) kèhù [ker-hoo]
  you're a very important customer nín shi wǒmen de zhòngdiǎn kèhù [neen shur wor-mun der joong-dyen ker-hoo]

Customs hǎiguān [hI-gwahn] 海关

D

dark àn [ahn]

date hào [how]

DATES

The basic words you will need to be able to ask or say the date in Chinese are:

nián	[nyen]	year
yuè	[yew-eh]	month
hào	[how]	day of the month

In the full form of the date these are all preceded by a number.

For example:

1 January 1988
yījiǔbābā nián yīyue yí hào
[yee-jyoh-bahbah nyeen yee-yew-eh yee-how] .

Note that the Chinese way of expressing the date is in the inverse order to the English. The above date in Chinese says literally:

1988 year first month first day

If you just want to refer to the month and the day you can say:

1 May
wǔyue yí hào (*Labour Day which is a public holiday*) [woo-yew-eh yee how]

1 October
shíyue yí hào (*National Day*) [shur-yew-eh yee how]

To ask the date you replace the numbers before **hào** with the word **jǐ**, for example:

what date is it?
jǐ hào le?
[jee how ler]

what date is it today?
jīntian jǐ hào?
[jin-tyen jee how]

See also MONTHS, NUMBERS.

daughter nǚ'ér [nyew-er]

day tiān [tyen]

DAYS OF THE WEEK

To form the words for the days of the week in Chinese you use the word for 'week' – which is **xīngqi** [sying-chee] – and follow it with the numbers from 1 to 6 for Monday to Saturday and the word **rì** [rur] or **tiān** [tyen] for Sunday:

Monday	xīngqiyī [sying-chee-yee]
Tuesday	xīngqi'èr [sying-chee-er]
Wednesday	xīngqisān [sying-chee-sahn]
Thursday	xīngqisì [sying-chee-sur]
Friday	xīngqiwǔ [sying-chee-woo]
Saturday	xīngqiliù [sying-chee-lyoh]
Sunday	xīngqitiān *or* xīngqirì [sying-chee-tyen *or* sying-chee-rur]

dead sǐ [sur]

deal: it's a deal! yì yán wéi dìng! [yee yen way ding!]

December shí'èryue [shur-er-yew-eh]

declare: I have nothing to declare wǒ méi yǒu yào bàoguān de dōngxi [wor may yoh yow bow-gwahn der doong-syee]

delay (*noun*) wándiǎn [wahn-dyen]
   the flight's been delayed fēijī wándiǎnle [fay-jee wahn-dyen-ler]

delicious hǎochī [how-chur]
   that was delicious zhēn hǎochī [jun how-chur]
   (*literally: really good eat*)

dentist yákē dàifu [yah-ker dI-foo]

dentures jiǎyá [jyah-yah]

DIALECTS

There are a great many regional varieties of spoken Chinese which are often loosely referred to as dialects. Some are as different from each other as, for example, Italian and Portuguese, and a villager from northern China would have great difficulty talking to his counterpart in the south.

The 'dialects' of the great plains of the north and centre of China are quite closely related to each other.

In the mountainous south and east there is a great deal of linguistic diversity and the main dialects spoken there are:

Cantonese or **guăngdōng huà** [gwahng-doong hwah], which is spoken in Guangdong province (the part of China just to the north of Hong Kong), in Hong Kong itself and by most Chinese living in Britain;

Hakka or **kèjiā huà**, which is spoken in villages in parts of Guangdong province although it originated in north China centuries ago;

Hokkien or **fújiàn huà**, the language of the south-eastern province of Fujian and also of many Chinese living in Malaysia;

Wu, which is spoken in the Shanghai region and neighbouring provinces.

As well as their own regional language most educated Chinese understand **Pŭtōnghuà**. **Pŭtōnghuà** [poo-toong-hwah], still sometimes called Mandarin in the West, is modern standard Chinese, based on the pronunciation and dialect of Beijing. Mandarin, the common language used by officials under the empire, is its historical predecessor. **Pŭtōnghuà** is already the main form of Chinese used by the mass media and since April 1987 has been the only language of broadcasting for anything other than at a very local level. Children are taught **Pŭtōnghuà** at school and the long-term aim is for it to be the national as well as the official language of China. People would then be effectively bilingual in their own regional language and in **Pŭtōnghuà**.

diarrhoea lā dùzi [lah doo-dzur]

diary rìjìběnr [rur-jee-bunr]

dictionary cídiăn [tsur-dyen]
  a **Chinese–English dictionary** Hàn Yīng cídiăn [hahn ying tsur-dyen]

difference bùtóng [boo-toong]
  the **main difference** zhŭyàode bùtóng [joo-yow-der boo-toong]
  it **doesn't make any difference** dōu yíyàng [doh yee-yahng]

different bùtóng [boo-toong]

difficult nán [nahn]

difficulty kùnnán [koon-nahn]

DIMINUTIVES

Chinese does not usually form diminutives. You can put the word **xiǎo** [syow] (small) in front of a surname as a friendly way to refer to a colleague (*see* ADDRESSING PEOPLE). For example:

xiǎo Lǐ
young Lǐ

The word **lǎo** [low] (old) can also be used before the surname in the same way.

dinner wǎnfàn [wahn-fahn]

DINNER

Foreign visitors staying in hotels may well have their main meal in the evening, but most Chinese take the main meal of the day at lunchtimes in the canteen of their workplace. In the evening they normally eat at 5 to 6.30, the exception being banquets. (*See* FOOD.)

direct zhíjiē [jur-jyeh]
 (*flight*) zhífēi [jur-fay]

director dǒngshì [doong-shur]

dirty zāng [dzahng]

disadvantage huàichu [hwI-choo]

discount (*noun*) zhékòu [jur-koh]

discussion tǎolùn [tow-loon]

dish (*plate*) diézi [dyeh-dzur]
 (*meal*) cài [tsI]

diskette ruǎnpán [rwahn-pahn]
 on diskette cúnpán [tsoon-pahn]

distance jùlí [jyew-lee]
 what's the distance from ... to ...? cóng ... dào ...
 yǒu duō yuǎn? [tsoong ... dow ... yoh dwor yew-ahn]

DISTANCE

The metric system is the one officially used in China, so distances are measured in **gōngli** [goong-lee] or kilometres. People still use the traditional Chinese unit of distance which is the **lǐ**, approximately equivalent to half a kilometre. The **yīnglǐ** or mile is not generally understood.

distribution (*of goods*) fēnpèi [fun-pay]

divorced líhūn [lee-hoon]

do zuò [dzwor]
    can I do that? néng xíng ma? [nung sying mah]
    can you do that for me, please? qǐng nín bāng wo zuò yíxia, hǎo ma? [ching neen bahng wor dzwor yee-syah how ma]
    what are you doing? nǐ gàn shéme? [nee gahn shun-mah]
    will this/that do? zhèige/nèige kéyi ma? [jay-ger/nay-ger ker-yee mah]

doctor yīsheng [yee-shung]　医生

DOCTORS
Doctors are employed at hospitals or clinics and Chinese in cities are usually members of a medical insurance scheme through their workplaces and can consult them free of charge. Any medical treatment needed by foreign visitors will be arranged by the organization responsible for looking after them. In areas open to foreign travel there are usually hospitals and clinics specially designated for dealing with foreigners. Doctors in these establishments are carefully chosen and often know some English.

document wénjiàn [wun-jyen]

door mén [mun]

double shuāng [shwahng]
    double room shuāngren jiān [shwahng-run jyen]

down xià [syah]
    the price has come down jiàgé jiàngle [jyah-ger jyahng-ler]

down payment yùfù dìngjīn [yew-foo ding-jin]

draft (*of agreement*) cǎo'àn [tsow'ahn]

dragon lóng [loong]

dress (*noun*) yīfu [yee-foo]
    (*frock*) liányīqún [lyen-yee-chyewn]
    See CLOTHES.

drink (*verb*) hē [her]
    (*alcoholic*) jiǔ [jyoh]
    would you like a drink? hē dianr jiǔ ba? [her dyenr jyoh bah]
    thanks, but I don't drink xièxie, wǒ bú huì hē jiǔ [syeh-syeh, wor boo hway her jyoh]

DRINKS

The most common drink in China is tea (**chá**), but some Chinese drink

kāishuǐ
[kI-shway]
boiled water

which is drunk hot. This is said to be good for the dry throat that often affects people in north China and is always available in flasks in hotel rooms. When it has cooled down it is called:

lěng kāishuǐ
[lung kI-shway]
cold boiled water

Chinese tend to feel that cold water is bad for you and tap water is never drunk without being boiled.

In summer Chinese drink millions of bottles of:

qìshuǐr
[chee-shway]
fizzy pop

which is available at roadside stalls, although this is now facing serious competition from the imported delights of:

kékoukělè
[ker-koh-ker-ler]
Coca-Cola

The mineral water from the Laoshan spring or:

Láoshān kuàngquánshuǐ
[low-shahn kwahng-chyew-ahn-shway]

is also popular as is the Cola made from it. Beer (**píjiǔ** [pee-jyoh]) is becoming more popular and more widely available (*see* ALCOHOL, BEER).

driving licence jiàshǐ zhízhào [jyah-shur jur-jow]

drunk (*adjective*) hēzuìle [her-dzway-ler]
See ALCOHOL.

DRUNKENNESS

It is most unusual to see a Chinese drunk in public and it is certainly not acceptable for a foreigner to be drunk. Chinese tend to drink, if at all, at private or family functions.

dry gān [gahn]

dry-cleaning gānxǐ [gahn-syee]
There are no special dry-cleaners in China but hotels can do dry-cleaning for you.

duck yā
    Peking duck Běijīng kǎo yā [bay-jing kow yah]

DUPLICATION

Duplication is fairly common in Chinese. It may be
used to add an element of polite suggestion when a
complete phrase is said twice:

    qǐng zuò, qǐng zuò
    [ching dzwor, ching dzwor]
    please do sit down

Repeating a word can also have the effect of giving a
statement a more tentative tone:

    kěyi kànkan ma?
    [ker-yee kahn-kahn ma]
    can I have a (quick) look?

and it can make an imperative less abrupt:

    nǐ wènwen láo Lǐ
    [nee wun-wun low lee]
    why don't you ask old Li?

    wait for me
    [dung-dung wor]
    děngdeng wǒ

Duplication can also add extra emphasis:

    ràng wo hǎohao kànkan
    [rahng wor how-how kahn-kahn]
    let me have a good look at it

    wǒmen shìshi kàn
    [wor-mun shur-shur kahn]
    we'll try

during zai . . . de shíhou [dzI . . . der shur-hoh]

E

each měi [may]
  each of them tāmen zhōng měi yígè [tah-mun joong may yee-ger]
  how much are they each? yíge yào duōshao qián? [yee-ger yow dwor-show chyen]

ear ěrduo [er-dwor]

early (*arrive*) zǎo [dzow]
  early in the morning yì zǎo

> The word **zǎo** can also be used to mean 'good morning'.

east dōng [doong]
  in the East dōngfang [doong-fahng]

Easter Fùhuójié [foo-hwor-jyeh]

EASTER
Like Christmas, Easter is of no significance to Chinese apart from the tiny minority who are practising Christians.

easy róngyì [roong-yee]

eat chī [chur]
  I would like something to eat wó xiǎng chī diǎnr dōngxi [wor syahng chur dyenr doong-syee]
  let's go and eat wǒmen chīfàn qù ba [wor-mun chur-fahn chyew bah]

> The word **fàn**, which originally meant 'cooked rice', now means food in general and should be used when you are using the word 'eat' without a particular object as in the second example above .

EATING HABITS
Most people are familiar with Chinese mealtime etiquette from Chinese restaurants in the West, and the rules in China are roughly the same. At a formal restaurant meal there will normally be one large bowl of rice (**mǐfàn** [mee-fahn]) and several fish, meat or vegetable dishes (**cài** [tsI]) in the centre of the table. Each diner has his or her own bowl and it is not necessary to take the different dishes in any particular order. Fish dishes tend to come late in the meal, and this is a useful indicator that the meal is drawing to a close. Leaving a small amount in the

bowl can be a sign that you have finished, i.e. you have no room for more.

Beer or fizzy orangeade, if ordered, will be served at the beginning of the meal. The soup normally comes at the end in the north of China, but Cantonese people prefer it first.

When eating in the Chinese dining-room of a hotel the same principles apply, but the rice (or rice gruel – **xīfàn** [syee-fahn] – at breakfast) will probably be in a large pot on a side table and the guest will be expected to help himself.

Chopsticks (**kuàizi** [kwI-dzur]) are the normal eating implements but are not completely universal. Lunch in office canteens in Beijing, for example, is often served in large enamel dishes and eaten with spoons. When soup is served it is more polite to drink it with a spoon, but it is also perfectly correct to drink from the bowl. (*See* CHOPSTICKS.)

Slurping noises are acceptable, particularly when eating noodles, and it is quite polite to raise a bowl of noodles or rice to the mouth. It is also more practical.

Although the hamburger restaurant has not yet colonized China as it has Japan, there is a growing fast-food industry, particularly in areas like the streets around the Imperial Palace in Beijing where large numbers of Chinese tourists congregate, and there are many stalls and small restaurants offering 'fast, homely food' (**kuàicān biànfàn**). Stalls in the East Wind market in central Beijing – the **Dōngfēng shìchǎng** [doong-fahng shur-chahng] – do a nice line in **bāozi** [bow-dzur] (steamed bread stuffed with meat etc. – four is the standard order) and trays of rice with a savoury topping for shoppers. (*See* RESTAURANTS.)

economy: the Chinese economy Zhōngguo jīngjì [joong-gwor jing-jee]

either: either one rènhé yíge [run-her yee-ger]
either . . . or . . . huòzhe . . . huòzhe . . . [hwor-jer]

electric diàn [dyen]

ELECTRICITY

Electricity in China is 220V and some cities are subject to a daily power cut or **tíngdiàn** to save resources. Large hotels use standby generators for this and you will also see generators in shops in

Guangzhou and other cities. Batteries are not always easily available outside the main cities.

electronics diànzǐxué [dyen-dzur-syew-eh]

else: do you want something else? hái yào shénme ma? [hI yow shun-mah mah]
  somewhere else biéde dìfang [byeh-der dee-fahng]

embarrassing shǐ rén bù hǎoyìsi [shur run boo how-yee-sur]

EMBARRASSMENT

The easiest way to avoid embarrassing your Chinese hosts is not to discuss taboo subjects. Anything to do with national defence should be avoided as should unsolicited criticism of the political system or the party leadership. It is quite possible that the Chinese you meet may have more radical views on these subjects than you, but it is impolite to insist on discussing these topics unless it is with someone you know well. Avoid discussing sexual topics, but do not be surprised to find that Chinese are more open than Westerners when it comes to talking about people's ages or about how much they earn. Insisting on doing something or going somewhere that your host does not want is also likely to cause embarrassment. *See also* LAUGHING.

embassy: the British embassy Yīngguó dàshíguǎn [ying-gwor dah-shur-gwahn]

empty (*adjective*) kōng [koong]

end (*noun: of road*) jìntóu [jin-toh]
  the end of the month yuèdǐ [yew-eh-dee]
  the end of the year niándǐ [nyen-dee]

England Yīngguó [ying-gwor]   英国
This word is also used to refer to the United Kingdom as a whole.

English (*adjective*) Yīngguó [ying-gwor]
  (*language*) Yīngyǔ [ying-yew]
  I'm English wǒ shi Yīngguo ren [wor shur ying-gwor run]
  do you speak English? ní jiǎng Yīngyǔ ma? [nee jyahng ying-yew mah]

ENGLISH

English is recognized as the 'number one foreign language', with Japanese running second. It is widely taught. The emphasis until recently has been on reading and writing, particularly for scientists and technologists of the older generation. The Chinese press has been lamenting the low level of spoken English but the situation is beginning to change. There is now an English Corner in the south-western part of Beijing's **Zǐzhúyuàn** [dzur-joo-yew-ahn] Park where teachers and students meet to speak English: it received a kind of official blessing with a visit from the British ambassador in 1987.

Learning English has become vitally important for the growing number of hotel and tourist staff and there was a cult following for the BBC English-by-TV series 'Follow Me'. Hotel staff are keen to practise their spoken English and visitors often find themselves giving impromptu English lessons over meals. (These should not be confused with 'English lessons' requested less openly and which have about the same linguistic content as 'French lessons' offered in Soho.)

In spite of the widespread interest in English, it cannot be overemphasized that the vast majority of people in China know no English at all and have never seen it written or heard it spoken. In the countryside you are most likely to be able to communicate in English with children, since they will be learning English at school. In the major cities and particularly in hotels it is possible to find English-speakers to help out, and host organizations and the Chinese Travel Service, **Lǚxíngshè** [lyew-sying-sher], can provide interpreters who are usually helpful.

enough gòu [goh]
  not enough bú gòu [boo goh]
  that's enough, thank you gòule, xièxie [goh-ler syeh-syeh]

entrance rùkǒu [roo-koh]   入口

envelope xìnfēng [syin-fung]

essential: that's essential nà shi bìyào de [nah shur bee-yow der]
  no, that's not essential nà bú shi bìyào de

estimate (*noun*) gūjì [goo-jee]
  it's only an estimate zhǐ shìge gūjì [jur shur-ger goo-jee]

Europe Ōuzhou [oh-joh]
  in Europe zai Ōuzhou [dzI oh-joh]

evening wǎnshang [wahn-shahng]
    this evening jīntian wǎnshang [jin-tyen wahn-shahng]
    good evening ní hǎo [nee how]
    Note that **ní hǎo** means 'hello' and is a greeting that can be used at any time of day.

every měige [may-ger]

everyone měige rén [may-ger run]
    hello everyone dàjiā hǎo [dah-jyah how]

everything měijiàn shìr [may-jyen shur]
    (*objects*) suóyǒu de dōngxi [swor-yoh der doong-syee]
    well, I think that's everything (*said at end of meeting etc.*) hǎo, wǒmen jiù kāi dào zhèr ba [how wor-mun jyoh kI dow jer bah]

excellent hǎojíle [how-jee-ler]
    excellent! hǎojíle!

exchange rate duìhuàn lǜ [dway-hwahn lyew]
    what is the exchange rate for the pound? yīngbàng de duìhuàn lǜ shi duōshao? [ying-bahng der dway-hwahn lyew shur dwor-show]

excuse me (*to get past*) máfan nín [mah-fahn neen]
    (*to get attention*) máfan nín, qǐng wèn . . . [mah-fahn neen ching wun]
    (*apology*) duìbuqǐ [dway-boo-chee]
    excuse me, could you tell me where . . .? máfan nín wèn yíxia, . . . zài nǎr? [mah-fahn neen wun yee-syah . . . dzI nar]

exhausted: I'm exhausted wǒ lèisile [wor lay-sur-ler]

exhibition (*trade fair etc.*) jiāoyì huì [jyow-yee hway]

exit chūkǒu [choo-koh] 出 口

expenses: it's on expenses wǒmen gōngsī fùqián [wor-mun goong-sur foo-chyen]
    travel expenses lǚfèi [lyew-fay]
    accommodation expenses fángfèi [fahng-fay]

expensive guì [gway]

expiry date (*of visa etc.*) shīxiào qī [shur-syow chee]

explain: could you explain that to me? qíng nǐ bāng wǒ jiěshì yíxia, hǎo ma? [ching nee bahng wor jyeh-shur yee-syah how mah]

export (*verb*) chūkŏu [choo-koh]
  we export . . . wŏmen chūkŏu . . .
  our export campaign wŏmen de chūkŏu yùndòng
  [wor-mun der choo-koh yewn-doong]

export director chūkŏubù dŏngshì [choo-koh-boo
  doong-shur]

express: by express mail kuàidì yóujiàn [kwI-dee yoh-
  jyen]

express train kuài chē [kwI cher]

expression (*on face*) liănsè [lyan-ser]

EXPRESSIONS (FACIAL)

Chinese people are restrained in their facial expressions and gestures, particularly when dealing with
foreigners, as long years of experience have taught
them that foreigners are not always to be trusted –
hence perhaps the notion of the 'inscrutable orien-
tal'. Once trust has been earned, however, people
will show their feelings much more openly. Chinese
may look away if they don't feel able to answer your
question or if they don't agree with what you say.
They may also laugh or look anxious when embarrassed. *See also* GESTURES.

extension: extension 334 (*telephone*) sānsānsì fēnjī
  [sahn-sahn-sur fun-jee]
  (*of contract*) yáncháng [yen-chahng]

extra: there are no extra charges bú zài lìngwài shōufèi
  [boo dzI ling-wI show-fay]
  is that extra? yào lìng fùqián ma? [yow ling foo-
  chyen mah]

eye yănjing [yen-jing]

F

face liǎn [lyen]

factory gōngchǎng [goong-chahng]

fair (*commercial*) shāngpǐn jiāoyìhuì [shahng-pin jyow-yi-hway]

fall (*verb*) (*person*) shuāidǎo [shwI-dow]
 sales are falling xiāoshòu liàng zai xiàdiē [syow-shoh lyahng dzI syah-dyeh]

family jiātíng [jyah-ting]
 my family wǒde jiātíng [wor-der jyah-ting]

FAMILY

Family connections are extremely important in China and it is not unusual for three generations to live in the same house and for the grandparents to play a major role in the upbringing of the children. Chinese people are far more particular than most Westerners about the precise definition of family relationships and use different words for aunt, for example, depending on whether she is their mother's sister, father's sister etc.

Here is a list of some common names for family members:

elder brother	gēge [ger-ger]
younger brother	dìdi [dee-dee]
elder sister	jiějie [jyeh-jyeh]
younger sister	mèimei [may-may]
mother	mǔqin [moo-chin]
father	fùqin [foo-chin]
son	érzi [er-dzur]
daughter	nǚ'ér [nyew-er]
aunt	
(*father's sister*)	gūgu [goo-goo]
(*mother's sister*)	yímǔ [yee-moo]
uncle	
(*father's elder brother*)	bāibai [bI-bI]
(*father's younger brother*)	shūshu [shoo-shoo]
(*mother's brother*)	jiùjiu [jyoh-jyoh]
son-in-law	nǚxù [nyew-syew]

daughter-in-law	érxí [er-syee]
grandson	
(*son's son*)	sūnzi [soon-dzur]
(*daughter's son*)	wàisūn [wI-soon]
granddaughter	
(*son's daughter*)	sūnnǚr [soon-nyewr]
(*daughter's daughter*)	wàisūnnǚr [wI-soon-nyewr]
grandfather	
(*paternal*)	yéye [yeh-yeh]
(*maternal*)	lǎoye [low-yeh]
grandmother	
(*paternal*)	nǎinai [nI-nI]
(*maternal*)	lǎolao [low-low]

far yuǎn [yew-ahn]
　how far is it to ...? dào ... yǒu duō yuǎn? [dow ... yoh dwor yew-ahn]
　is it far? yuǎn bù yuǎn? (*literally: far not far?*)

Far East Yuǎndōng [yew-ahn-doong]
　This is not a popular term as it implies a Eurocentric view of the world. The Chinese would rather think of themselves as being in **Dōng Yà** or East Asia.

fast kuài [kwI]
　too fast tài kuài

father fùqin [foo-chin]

FATHER
　In an urban family the word **bàba** [bah-bah], equivalent to 'dad', is often used, whereas in a rural family **diē** or **dǎda** is more common.

faulty (*equipment*) yǒu máobìng [yoh mow-bing]

fax (*noun*) chuánzhēn [chwahn-jun]

February èryue [er-yew-eh]

FEC *see* FOREIGN EXCHANGE CERTIFICATES.

feel: how are you feeling? nǐ juéde zěnmeyàng le? [nee jew-eh-der zun-mah-yahng ler]
　I'm feeling better wo háo diǎnr le [wor how dyenr ler]
　I feel like a ... (*drink etc.*) wó xiǎng ... [wor syahng]

ferry bǎidù [bI-doo]

FESTIVALS

In the days of the empire the passing of the seasons was marked by many festivals. Most of these have died out, but some important ones survive. Their dates are calculated according to the traditional lunar calendar, so they fall on different days each year. Chinese New Year, the Spring Festival, is by far the most important, so that is dealt with separately (*see* NEW YEAR). The other important festivals are:

Qīngmíng [ching-ming] or 'Clear and Bright Festival' is celebrated in early April. This is the time for families to come together to tend the graves of their ancestors. They go out to the graveyard, often taking a picnic, sweep and tidy the graves, and burn paper money for the spirits of the dead. Since the revolution of 1949 this traditional ceremony has been merged with the commemoration of those who died in the service of the Chinese revolution and the leaders of China who have died in recent years.

Yuánxiāo Jié [yew-ahn-syow jyeh] or the Lantern Festival takes place two weeks after the Spring Festival and is the formal end to the Spring Festival celebrations. Firecrackers and coloured lanterns appear everywhere and **yuánxiāo** – sweet and sticky rice flour dumplings – are eaten. People try to prolong the Spring Festival celebrations right up to the Lantern Festival by keeping the family together and feasting, if they can. Westerners should avoid trying to do business with Chinese during this period as their hearts will not really be in it.

The **Duānwǔ** [dwahn-woo] Festival or Dragon Boat Festival takes place in late May or early June. It commemorates the death by drowning of Qu Yuan, a great poet and virtuous official of the fourth century BC. Dragon Boat races symbolize the search for his body, and sticky rice cakes are eaten in memory of offerings made by fishermen to the river god.

Zhòngqiū [joong-chyoh] or The Mid-autumn Festival in late September or early October can be traced back to ancient ceremonies of moon worship. These days it is celebrated by going out to some vantage point to view the full moon and, in some parts of China, by eating stodgy 'moon cakes' (they are round like the moon) with sweet bean or savoury fillings.

All these festivals are celebrated by the majority, **Hàn**, Chinese nationality. The ethnic minorities all have festivals of their own.

few jǐ [jee]
    a few days jǐ tiān [jee tyen]
    just a few jiù jǐge [jyoh jee-ger]

figure (*number*) shùzì [shoo-dzur]
    can we see the figures? wǒmen kànyikàn shùzì, xíng ma? [wor-mun kahn-yee-kahn shoo-dzur sying mah]

filling: I need a filling wǒde yá gāi bǔ le [wor-der yah gI boo ler]

film (*for camera*) jiāojuǎnr [jyow jyew-ahnr]
    (*at cinema*) diànyǐng [dyen-ying]

final zuìhòu [dzway-hoh]
    that's our final offer nà shi wǒmen zuìhòu de bàojià [nah shur wor-mun dzway-hoh der bow-jyah]

finance director cáiwù dǒngshì [tsI-woo doong-shur]

find zhǎodào [jow-dow]

fine: that's fine hǎo [how]

finger shóuzhǐ [shoh-jur]

finish: I haven't finished wǒ hái méi gànwán [wor hI may gahn-wahn]
    when does it finish? shénme shíhou néng wán? [shun-mah shur-hoh nung wahn]

To express the idea of 'having finished doing something' Chinese places the suffix **wán** after the relevant verb. For example:

    eat – chī
    I have finished eating
    wǒ chīwán le
    [wor chur-wahn ler]
    I haven't finished eating
    wǒ hái méi chīwán
    [wor hI may chur-wahn]
    read – kàn
    he's finished reading it
    tā kànwán le
    [tah kahn-wahn ler]
    we'll finish the job next month
    wǒmen xiàge yuè jiù gànwán le
    [wor-mun syah-ger yew-eh jyoh gahn-wahn ler]

the job is almost finished
kuài gànwán le
[kwI gahn-wahn ler]

fire (*for heating*) huǒ [hwor]
  (*destructive*) huǒzāi [hwor-dzI]

first (*adjective*) dìyī [dee-yee]
  See DATES.

first class (*travel etc.*) yīděng [yee-dung]

FIRST CLASS

The word **yīděng** is used for travel by ship or by plane. On trains you have the choice of:

ruǎnwò
[rwahn-wor]
soft berth

which is the most expensive, or:

ruǎnzuò
[rwahn-dzwor]
soft seat

and:

yìngwò
[ying-wor]
hard berth

which is the same price as soft seat, and:

yìngzuò
[ying-zwor]
hard seat

which is the cheapest.

first name míngzi [ming-dzur]

FIRST NAMES

Chinese given names or **míngzi** come after the surname so are not really 'first' names. They are also called 'given names'. The meanings of the names were traditionally supposed to convey qualities to the children, so girls' names might include the characters for 'beautiful' or the names of flowers or trees, and boys' names would indicate wisdom, learning and strength.

Examples of girls' names are:

Lì
[lee]
beautiful (*not to be confused with the surname Lǐ*)

Yùlán
[yew-lahn]

magnolia

Guìfāng

[gway-fahn]

cassia fragrance (*the flower of a plant related to the laurel*)

Some examples of boys' names are:

Sīcōng

[sur-tsoong]

wisdom

Wén

[wun]

learning

Lì

[lee]

strength

The last boys' name, **Lì**, is written with a completely different character from the girls' name **Lì**. A Chinese person seeing the character would immediately know if **Lì** was a male or a female name – but it is not clear from the Pinyin. The interesting thing is that educated people prefer to choose names which are not obviously male or female.

The politicization of everyday life since 1949 has spread to names and some now have national or political significance. For example, somebody might have the given name:

Jiěfàng

[jyeh-fahng]

liberation

to commemorate the victory of the Communist Party.

Shènglì

[shung-lee]

victory

is another political name which might commemorate the 1949 victory or any military or political triumph.

The name:

Jiànguó

[jyen-gwor]

foundation of the state

refers to the establishment of the People's Republic of China in 1949.

Kàngměi

[kahng-may]

resist America

dates from China's support for the North Koreans in
the Korean war from 1950.

Chāoyīng
[chow-ying]
surpass Britain

stems from the time when China was attempting to
increase its industrial production to overtake Britain.

It is important to remember that given names are
only used to small children or close friends and it is
best never to use them unless you are specifically
asked to. *See* ADDRESSING PEOPLE.

fish (*noun*) yú [yew]

flat (*apartment*) dānyuán [dahn-yew-ahn]

flight hángbān [hahng-bahn]
my flight is at ... wǒde fēijī ... fēi [wor-der fay-jee
... fay]

flight number hángbān hào [hahng-bahn how]

floor (*wooden*) dìbǎn [dee-bahn]
(*concrete*) dì
(*in hotel etc.*) céng [tsung]
on the third/fourth floor zai sāncéng/sìcéng [dzI san-
tsung/sur-tsung]

Note that **yīcéng** (*literally: first floor*) is what we in
Britain call the ground floor; Chinese usage parallels
American usage in starting at the first floor.

flower huā [hwah]
a bunch of flowers yíshù huā [yee-shoo hwah]

flu liúgǎn [lyoh-gahn]

fly (*verb*) fēi [fay]

food shíwù [shur-woo]
(*colloquial word*) chīde [chur-der]

FOOD

Chinese food is one of the great cuisines of the
world. It varies enormously from north to south and
from region to region. Northerners tend to go for
wheat-based staples such as steamed bread (**mántou**
[mahn-toh]) and noodles whereas in the south rice
(**mǐfàn** [mee-fahn]) is the essential accompaniment.
Northern food tends to be bland and the northerners
do not particularly like the sweet and vinegary
flavours of southern, especially Cantonese, cooking.
Eastern China includes many sea and river fish in its
dishes and the Sichuan and Hunan provinces of

south-western and central China are noted for spicy and peppery food with plenty of chillies. Chinese Muslims have their own cuisine and special restaurants and cafés, which often have signs in Arabic script above the door.

Everyday cooking tends to be filling and simple. Decades of rural poverty bred frugality and ingenuity. The most important part of a meal is the rice, bread or noodle staple to which different dishes (**cài** [tsI]) are added for taste and a more varied diet. These are often mostly vegetable. In the past meat was scarce and expensive and it is still traditional in China to save meat for celebrations and festivals. Vegetarian food (**sùcài** [soo-tsI]) is not uncommon and this is connected with Buddhist beliefs.

Here is a selection of some of the commoner Chinese dishes:

HORS D'OEUVRES (*cold platters*)

pīnpánr [pin-pahnr]
    cold platter

shíjǐn lěngpánr [lung-pahnr]
    assorted cold platter

PORK

yúxiāng ròusī [yew-syahng roh-sur]
    stir-fried shredded pork in hot spicy sauce

gōngbǎo ròudīng [goong-bow roh-ding]
    stir-fried diced pork with peanuts and chilli

jiàngbào lǐjī [jyahng-bow lee-jee]
    pork fillet quick-fried with bean sauce

huáliū ròupiànr [hwah-lyoh roh-pyenr]
    stir-fried sliced pork with thick sauce added

gúlǎo ròu [goo-low roh]
    sweet and sour pork

tángcù páigǔ [tahng-tsoo pI-goo]
    sweet and sour spare ribs

huíguō ròu [hway-gwor roh]
    twice-cooked pork (boiled then stir-fried)

hóngshāo ròu [hoong-show roh]
    diced pork braised in brown (sweet and soya) sauce

mùxū ròu [moo-syew roh]
    stir-fried sliced pork with eggs, tree-ear (a type of edible fungus) and day lily (dried lily)

bǎnlì shāoròu [bahn-lee show-roh]
    pork braised with chestnuts

shīzi tóu [shur-dzur toh]
    'lion head' (a large meatball stewed with cabbage)

jiàngbào sānyàng [jyahng-bow sahn-yahng]
    pork, pig's liver and kidney quick-fried with bean sauce

BEEF AND LAMB

cōngbào niúròu/yángròu [tsoong-bow nyohroh/yahng-roh]
    beef/lamb quick-fried with Chinese onions

málà niúròu [mah-lah nyoh-roh]
    stir-fried beef with chilli and wild pepper

gāli niúròu [gah-lee nyoh-roh]
    curried beef

háoyóu niúròu [how-yoh nyoh-roh]
    stir-fried beef with oyster sauce

dēngyǐng niúròu [dung-ying nyoh-roh]
    'lamp shadow beef' (spicy hot beef, steamed then deep-fried)

shuàn yángròu [shwahn yahng-roh]
    Mongolian hot-pot

kǎo yángròu chuànr [kow yahng-roh chwahnr]
    kebabs

POULTRY

Běijīng kǎo yā [bay-jing kow yah]
    Peking duck

zhāngchá yāzi [jahng-chah yah-dzur]
    whole duck smoked with tea and camphor leaves

xiāngsū yā/jī [syahng-soo ya/jee]
    crispy deep-fried whole duck/chicken

gōngbǎo jīdīng [goong-bow jee-ding]
    stir-fried diced chicken with peanuts and chilli

fúróng jīpiànr [foo-roong jee-pyenr]
    chicken slices with egg white

qìguō jī [chee-gwor jee]
    whole chicken steamed in a pot

jiàohua jī [jyow-hwah jee]
    'beggar's chicken' (charcoal-baked marinated chicken)

guàiwèir jī [gwI-wayr jee]
    'strange-tasting chicken' (whole chicken with peanuts and pepper)

fó tiào qiáng [foh tyow chyahng]
    'Buddha leaps the wall' (chicken with duck, pig's trotters and seafood in rice wine)

SEAFOOD

sōngshǔ huángyú [soong-shoo hwahng-yew]
sweet and sour crispy deep-fried croaker

tángcù yú [tahng-tsoo yew]
sweet and sour fish

qīngzhēng shíyú [ching-jung shur-yew]
steamed hilsa herring

hóngshāo lǐyú [hoong-show lee-yew]
carp braised in brown sauce

gānshāo guìyú [gahn-show gway-yew]
Chinese perch braised with chilli and bean sauce

qiézhī yúqiú [chyeh-jur yew-chyoh]
deep-fried fish balls with tomato sauce

sānsī yúchì [sahn-sur yew-chur]
shark's fin with shredded sea cucumber, abalone
(type of shellfish) and bamboo shoots

hóngpá hǎishēn [hoong-pah hI-shun]
sea cucumber stewed in brown sauce

liǎngchī dàxiā [lyahng-chur dah-syah]
'two-eat king prawns' (prawn heads deep-fried
and bodies stir-fried)

fúróng xiārénr [foo-roong syah-runr]
stir-fried shrimps with egg white

dàsuàn gānbèi [dah-swahn gahn-bay]
stir-fried scallops with garlic

cōngbào hǎiluó [tsoong-bow hI-lwor]
conch quick-fried with Chinese onion

háoyóu bāoyú [how-yoh bow-yew]
stir-fried abalone (type of shellfish) with oyster
sauce

bōjiǎo yōuyú [boh-jyow yoh-yew]
squid with spinach-wrapped minced meat

yúxiāng lóngxiā [yew-syahng loong-syah]
stir-fried lobster in hot spicy sauce

BEAN CURD (TOFU)

mápó dòufu [mah-poh doh-foo]
'pock-marked woman bean curd' (bean curd
with minced beef in hot spicy sauce)

málà dòufu [mah-lah doh-foo]
bean curd with chilli and wild pepper

jiācháng dòufu [jyah-chahng doh-foo]
home-style bean curd

shāguō dòufu [shah-gwor doh-foo]
bean curd in hot pot

guōtā dòufu [gwor-tah doh-foo]
bean curd fried in batter

GAME

fúróng yànwō [foo-roong yen-wor]
bird's nest with egg white

hóngshāo xióngzhǎng [hoong-show syoong-jahng]
bear's paw braised in brown sauce

sānxiān hóutóu [sahn-syen hoh-toh]
'three-fresh monkey head' (giant mushroom
with three other ingredients)

guōchǎo ānchúndàn [gwor-chow ahn-choon-dahn]
quail eggs on a vegetable base

xiānsǔn chǎo gēpiànr [syen-soon chow ger-pyenr]
stir-fried pigeon slices with bamboo shoots

shāojītuǐ bìng tiánjītuǐ [show-jee-tway bing tyen-jee-tway]
braised frogs' legs and chicken legs

dùn chuānshānjiǎ [doon chwahn-shahn-jyah]
braised pangolin (please refuse this dish as
pangolin – a kind of anteater – is an endangered
species!)

VEGETABLES

sù shíjǐn [soo shur-jin]
stir-fried assorted vegetables and meat

qīngjiāo chǎo ròupiànr [ching-jyow chow roh-pyenr]
stir-fried green pepper with sliced pork

shuāng gū chǎo sǔn [shwahng goo chow soon]
stir-fried mushrooms with bamboo shoots

jīyóu càixīn [jee-yoh tsIsyin]
stir-fried oilseed rape in chicken fat

xiānmó càihuā [syen-moh tsI-hwah]
stir-fried cauliflower with mushroom

nǎiyóu lóngxūcài [nI-yoh loong-syew-tsI]
stir-fried asparagus with cream

háimǐ báicài [hI-mee bI-ts'eye]
stir-fried Chinese cabbage with dried shrimps

shāo èr dōng [show er doong]
stir-fried mushroom and bamboo shoots with
vegetables

SOUP

shíjǐn dōngguā zhōng [shur-jin doong-gwah joong]
soup in winter marrow

suānlà tāng [swahn-lah tahng]
hot and sour soup

mùxū tāng [moo-syew tahng]
soup with sliced pork, eggs, tree-ear (a type of edible fungus) and day lily (dried lily)

xīhóngshì jīdàn tāng [syee-hoong-shur jee-dahn tahng]
soup with eggs and tomato

zhàcài ròusī tāng [jah-tsI roh-sur tahng]
soup with shredded pork and pickled mustard greens

bōcài fěnsī tāng [boh-tsI fun-sur tahng]
soup with spinach and vermicelli

sānxiān tāng [sahn-syen tahng]
'three-fresh' soup (soup with three particular ingredients varying from dish to dish)

kāishuǐ báicài [kI-shway bI-tsI]
Chinese cabbage in clear soup

zǐcài tāng [dzur-tsI tahng]
soup with zicai, dried shrimps etc. (zicai is an edible seaweed)

RICE, NOODLES, BREAD ETC.

mǐfàn [mee-fahn]
rice

xīfàn [syee-fahn]
rice porridge, congee

chǎofàn [chow-fahn]
fried rice

mántou [mahn-toh]
steamed bread

miàntiáor [myen-toh-r]
noodles

chǎomiàn [chow-myen]
fried noodles

huājuǎnr [hwah-jew-ahnr]
steamed roll

shuǐjiǎo [shway-jyow]
Chinese ravioli

zhēngjiǎo [jung-jyow]
steamed Chinese ravioli

guōtiē [gwor-tyeh]
fried Chinese ravioli

bāozi [bow-dzur]
baozi (steamed dumplings with various fillings, normally including minced pork)

shāomài [show-mI]
shaomai (steamed dumplings with wrapping

gathered on the top, containing various fillings, normally minced pork etc.)

chāshāobāo [chah-show-bow]
chashaobao (steamed dumplings with barbecued pork filling)

xiǎolóngbāo [syow-loong-bow]
xiaolongbao (steamed dumplings with various fillings, normally including minced pork, served on the bamboo steamers in which they have been cooked)

húntun (or **yúntún**) [hoon-toon]
wonton (smaller Chinese ravioli in soup)

cōngyóubǐng [tsoong-yoh-bing]
Chinese onion pancake

miànbāo [myen-bow]
bread (white)

hēi miànbāo [hay-myen-bow]
brown bread

SWEETS

básī píngguǒ/shānyào [bah-sur ping-gwor/shahn-yow]
apple/yam fritter

bābǎo fàn [bah-bow fahn]
'eight-treasure' rice pudding (with eight kinds of fruit and nuts)

sān bù zhān [sahn boo jahn]
'three non-stick' (sweets made from egg yolk, mung bean powder etc., so called because they don't stick to plate, chopsticks or teeth)

bīngtáng yín'ěr [bing-tahng yin-er]
silver tree-ear (type of edible fungus) in syrup

xìngrénr dòufu [sying-runr doh-foo]
almond 'bean curd' (almond paste dessert)

liánzi gēng [lyen-dzur gung]
lotus-seed in syrup

shíjǐn shuíguo gēng [shur-jin shway-gwor gung]
fruit salad

xīgua zhōng [syee-gwah joong]
assorted fruit in watermelon

wāndòuhuáng [wahn-doh-hwahng]
sweet pea cake

bōluo láozāo [boh-lwor low-dzow]
pineapple in fermented glutinous rice

SNACKS

yóutiáo [yoh-tyow]
   unsweetened doughnut sticks

dòujiāng (or **dòuzhī**) [doh-jyahng, doh-jur]
   soya bean milk

yóubǐng [yoh-bing]
   deep-fried savoury pancake

xiànrbǐng [syenr-bing]
   savoury fritter

shāobǐng [show-bing]
   sesame pancake

dòushā sūbǐng [doh-shah soo-bing]
   baked flaky cake with sweet bean paste filling

huǒshāo [hwor-show]
   baked wheaten bun

táng huǒshāo [tahng hwor-show]
   baked wheaten bun with sugar

yóuzhágāo [yoh-jah-gow]
   deep-fried sweet pancake

dòushābāo [doh-shah-bow]
   steamed dumpling with sweet bean paste filling

chūnjuǎnr [choon-jyew-ahnr]
   spring rolls

See also FRUIT.

foot (*on body*) jiǎo [jyow]

for: this is for you zhè shi géi nǐde [jay shur gay nee-der]
   that's for me nà shi géi wǒde [na shur gay wor-der]
   are you for the idea? nǐ tóngyì ma? [nee toong-yee mah]
   for three nights (*e.g. room*) wǒ zhù sānge wǎnshang [wor joo sahn-ger wahn-shahng]

Forbidden City Gùgōng [goo-goong]

foreign wàiguo [wI-gwor]

foreign exchange (*money*) wàihuì [wI-hway]

foreign exchange certificate wàihuì juànr [wI-hway jyew-ahnr]

FOREIGN EXCHANGE CERTIFICATES (FECs)

FECs are the 'funny money' that tourists and foreign residents are supposed to use instead of 'real' money or **Rénmínbì** [run-min-bee] (*see* MONEY). Technically they are just a receipt to indicate that an equivalent amount of foreign currency has been brought into China. In the major tourist hotels and Friendship stores only FECs are accepted – the rationale being that scarce luxury goods are sold only if they bring in foreign currency. This, however, makes FECs highly desirable and you can exchange them at a premium for **Rénmínbì** from shady characters who will stop you in the street with their only English phrase 'change money'. In Beijing the Uighurs from Xinjiang province have the reputation for being the most active in this. Changing FECs into **Rénmínbì** this way is illegal, although however hard you try you will acquire some RMB in change. You can spend this in shops but it is best to get some small denomination FECs when you change your traveller's cheques. There is a long-standing rumour in China that FECs are about to be abolished and this could happen at any time.

Some useful phrases are:

no, I don't want to (i.e. to change my FECs)
wǒ bú huàn [wor boo hwahn]
(*literally: I not change*)

can I have some small denomination FECs, please?
qǐng huàn diǎnr língde, hǎo ma?
[ching hwahn dyenr ling-der how mah]

In the first example here note the typical Chinese tendency to express only the very minimum that is necessary.

foreigner wàiguo ren [wI-gwor run]

FOREIGNERS
Wàiguo ren is the formal word for 'foreigner' but the Chinese have a range of expressions to refer to foreigners, some more complimentary than others. One commonly used expression is:

dà bízi
[dah bee-dzur]
big nose

Another is:

yáng guǐzi
[yahng gway-dzur]
foreign devil

Dictionaries published in China say that this is a term used in 'pre-liberation China for foreign invaders', but if you keep your ears pinned back while walking around in China you will hear people muttering '**yáng guïzi**' under their breath.

Another expression:

hóng máozi
[hoong mow-dzur]
redheads

goes back at least as far as the mid nineteenth century and is still used by some Chinese, including the Hakkas from the south.

lăo wài
[low wI]
(*literally: old foreigner*)

is a friendly and respectful term rapidly gaining currency.

There are less complimentary terms. For example, the British may be referred to as:

Yīngguo lăo
[ying-gwor low]

This is not very polite, the nearest equivalent being the American 'limey' or the Australian 'pom'.

forget wàng [wahng]
   I forget wŏ wàngle [wor wahng-ler]
   I didn't forget wŏ méi wàng [wor may wahng]
   I forgot to bring my passport wŏ wàngle dài hùzhào le [wor wahn ler dI hoo-jow ler]

fork (*for eating*) chāzi [chah-dzur]

FORKS

There is no problem getting a fork (and knife) in the Western food restaurants of the major hotels, but don't expect to get them in the ordinary restaurants where most Chinese eat. You will have to use chopsticks like everyone else there.

formal (*dinner, occasion*) zhènshì [jun-shur]

FORMALITY

Banquets and meetings are always arranged to a set formula, but that does not necessarily mean that people behave stiffly.

free (*no cost*) miăn fèi [myen fay]

freight (*noun*) huòwù [hwor-woo]

Friday xīngqiwŭ [sying-chee-woo]

fridge bīngxiāng [bing-syahng]

fried rice chăofàn [chow-fahn]

friend péngyou [pung-yoh]

FRIENDS
Chinese people take friendships very seriously and friendship involves considerable obligations on both sides. Lasting friendships are often made at school, college or university, and there is a special word in Chinese – **tóngxué** [toong-syew-eh] – meaning 'fellow student' to describe people who you have a connection with because you were at school or university together, but who are not necessarily close personal friends. If people meet decades after graduation and discover that they are **lăo tóngxué** an immediate rapport is established.

Friendship (**yŏuyì** [yoh-yee]) has also become a cliché for the relations between countries and is a safe subject for toasts at banquets:

wèi wŏmen liăngguó rénmin de yŏuyì, gān bēi!
[way wor-muń lyahng-gwor run-min der yoh-yee gahn-bay]
to the friendship of our two peoples!

Chinese prefer to deal with people they know, whether it is in commercial or official business, and the term **lăo péngyou** – old friend – is usually applied to someone they have dealt with before and whose credentials have already been established. *See* CONNECTIONS.

friendship store yŏuyí shāngdiàn [yoh-yee shahng-dyen]

FRIENDSHIP STORES
These are large, well-equipped department stores cum supermarkets in the larger cities intended specifically for expatriate foreign residents such as diplomats and journalists, and tourists. They sell Western goods not available in ordinary shops – instant coffee, teabags and Scotch whisky for example – luxury items and high-quality handicrafts. Goods can be paid for only in Foreign Exchange Certificates or by credit card, so the vast majority of the Chinese are excluded from them, and even if they acquire some FECs they are likely to be turned away by the police or security guards.

from cóng [tsoong]
I've come from ... wŏ shi cóng ... lái de [wor shur tsoong ... ll der]
from Monday to Wednesday cóng xīngqiyī dào

xīngqiwù [tsoong sying-chee-yee dow sying-chee-woo]

from next month cóng xiège yuè qǐ [tsoong syeh-ger yew-eh chee]

(*when distance is described*) lí [lee]

5 kilometres from here lí zhèr wǔ gōngli [lee jer woo goong-lee]

this is a present from us zhè shi wǒmen sòng nǐ de lǐwù [jay shur wor-mun soong nee der lee-woo]

front: in front of . . . . . . qiánmian [chyen-myen]
in front of the hotel fàndiàn qiánmian

fruit shuíguǒ [shway-gwor]

FRUIT

Fruit is widely available and varies from region to region. Southern China produces tropical fruits such as mangoes and pineapples, and the persimmon, lichee and longan are popular. Apples, oranges and other fruits common in the West are on sale – served at the end of formal restaurant meals. All fruit in China is peeled before being eaten as it will almost all have been sprayed with pesticides. The most popular summer fruit is the ubiquitous watermelon which is on sale on every street corner. When there is a watermelon glut, the newspapers are full of articles on different ways of eating them to encourage people to buy more, and on the problems of disposing of the thousands of tons of peel. In fact many of the litter bins you see on the street are labelled 'fruit peel'!

> **guǒ pí xiāng** 果皮箱

Here is a list of common Chinese fruit:

apple	píngguo [ping-gwor]
apricot	xìngzi [sying-dzur]
banana	xiāngjiāo [syahn-jyow]
cherry	yīngtao [ying-tow]
grape	pútao [poo-tow]
Hami melon	hāmìguā [hahmee-gwah] (*yellow, similar to honeydew*)
haw	shānzhā [shahn-jah] (*hawthorn berry, sour-tasting, dark red fruit with smooth skins, popular with health food enthusiasts as it is believed to be good for high blood pressure and heart disease*)

kumquat	jīnjú [jeen-jyew] (*small sharp-tasting oranges*)
lichee	lìzhī [lee-jur] (*plum-sized fruit with brown bumpy hard skin and white juicy fragrant flesh*)
longan	lóngyăn [loong-yen] (*white flesh, like an oak-apple in size and colour, similar to lichee*)
mandarin orange	gānzi [gahn-dzur]
melon	xiāngguā [syahng-gwah]
peach	táozi [tow-dzur]
pear	lí [lee]
persimmon	shìzi [shur-dzur] (*large, soft, yellow, sweet-tasting fruit*)
pineapple	bōluo [boh-lwor]
plum	lĭzi [lee-dzur]
pomegranate	shíliu [shur-lyoh]
tangerine	júzi [jyew-dzur]
watermelon	xīguā [syee-gwah]

full (*hotel*) kè măn [ker mahn]
  no thanks, I'm full búyàole, wŏ chībăole [boo-yow-ler wor chur-bow-ler]

fun: it's fun hén hăowánr [hun how-wahnr]

funny (*strange*) qíguài [chee-gwI]
  (*comical*) huáji [hwah-jee]

furniture jiājù [jyah-jyew]

FURNITURE

Traditional Chinese furniture was at its best an important art form and came in many elaborate designs. Modern houses and flats, however, are rather sparsely furnished by Western standards, disposable incomes still being relatively low. In recent years the amount and range of furniture on sale has increased and anyone strolling around Beijing can see small businesses producing simple but sturdy tables, chairs and cupboards. Some of the cane furniture on sale in the street markets is very fine.

Hotel rooms tend to be furnished in a standard international style, but provincial hotels seem very old-fashioned in comparison with the modern Joint Venture hotels in Beijing and Guangzhou.

further: is it much further? hái hén yuăn ma? [hI hun yew-ahn mah]

future jiānglái [jyahng-lI]
   in future jiānglái

FUTURE TENSE

Chinese does not place the same emphasis on tenses that European languages do. The sentence:

   tā qù

can mean: he goes
or: he is going
or: he will go

depending on the context. The verb **qù** remains unchanged, since Chinese verbs do not take endings. If it is necessary to indicate that an action is going to take place at some future time then a 'time word' included in the sentence will usually make the meaning clear:

   tā míngtian qù
   he is going tomorrow

   ta qīyue qù
   he is going in July

G

gap: a gap in the market hái méi yǒu kāituò de shìchǎng [hI may yoh kI-toh der shur-chahng]

garage (*for petrol*) jiāyóu zhàn [jyah-yoh jahn]
See PETROL STATIONS.

garden huāyuán [hwah-yew-ahn]

garlic dàsuàn [dah-swahn]

gas (*for cooker etc.*) méiqì [may-chee]

GENDER

As in English, Chinese nouns do not have genders in the grammatical sense.

gents (*toilet*) nán cèsuǒ [nahn tser-swor]

GESTURES

Chinese tend to be as restrained in their gestures as in their facial expressions. There are few Western gestures that are likely to be misunderstood in China, but it is worth remembering that it is not done to throw your arms around a member of the opposite sex as a greeting.

Some particularly Chinese gestures are pointing the little finger downwards to indicate that something is bad, putting the tongue out to show that you have done something wrong or have made a faux pas and moving the hands across each other in front of you to mean emphatically no.
See also SHAKING HANDS.

get: where can I get . . .? (*buy*) zài nǎr kéyi mǎi . . .? [dzI nahr ker-yee mI]
have you got . . .? ní yǒu méi yǒu . . .? [nee yoh may yoh]
I haven't got . . . wó méi yǒu . . .
how do I get there? wó zěnme qù? [wor zun-mah chyew]
how do I get to . . .? wǒ zěnme qù . . .?
will you tell me when to get off? gāi xiàche de shíhou, jiào wǒ yíxia, hǎo ma? [gI syah-cher der shur-hoh jyow wor yee-syah how mah]
we'll get back to you on that nèijiàn shìr, wǒmen

yǐhòu zài liánxì [nay-jyen shur wor-mun yee-hoh dzI lyen-syee]

gift lǐwù [lee-woo]

GIFTS

China is not a gift-exchanging society like Japan and presenting large or expensive gifts to individuals (apart of course from personal friends) is likely to cause embarrassment. The recipients will have to hand them in to their organization. Token gifts or presentations from one organization to another are quite acceptable and are likely to be reciprocated with pleasure.

The sort of things that are likely to be appreciated are books, particularly illustrated ones, foreign stamps, cassettes of classical or popular music, perfumes, baseball caps, ties or women's head-scarves, foreign cigarettes, possibly a bottle of whisky – but it would be wise to check first whether the recipient would like one – key rings, particularly if they have a company logo or some other decoration, and anything to do with your company or the town or city in which it is located. Postcards, fibre or felt-tip pens, badges and T-shirts will go down well with youngsters.

girl nǚ háir [nyew hI-r]

give gěi [gay]
please give me . . . qǐng géi wǒ . . . [ching gay wor]

glass (*for drinking*) bōli bēi [boh-lee bay]
(*material*) bōli

glasses (*spectacles*) yǎnjìng [yen-jing]

gloves shǒutào [shoh-tow]

go qù [chyew]
tomorrow I'm going to . . . wǒ míngtian qù . . . [wor ming-tyen chyew]
I went there yesterday wǒ zuótian qù de nàr [wor dzwor-tyen chyew der nar]
where are you going? nǐ qù nǎr? [nee chyew nar]

gold (*colour*) jīnsè [jin-ser]
(*metal*) huángjīn [hwahng-jin]

good hǎo [how]
that's very good nà hén hǎo [nah hun how]

goodbye zàijiàn [dzI-jyen]
This means literally 'again see'.

GOODBYE
It is sometimes difficult to say goodbye to people on formal occasions. After a visit, a banquet or a meeting, the host will usually see you to the door. The guest should say:

> **qǐng liú bù**
> [ching lyoh boo]
> please don't bother to see me out

The host may well continue ushering you out, but when finally taking his leave you may hear him say:

> **mànzǒu**
> [mahn-dzoh]
> take care

More informally people might just say:

> **zǒu le?**
> [dzoh ler]

which means literally:
> you're off then?

to someone who is leaving the office.

goods huòwù [hwor-woo]

government zhèngfǔ [jung-foo]

grateful: we're very grateful wǒmen fēicháng gǎnxiè
[wor-mun fay-chahng gahn-syeh]

great (*tremendous*) hǎojíle [how-jee-ler]
that's really great! tài hǎo le! [tI how ler]

green lǜsède [lyew-ser-der]

GREETINGS *see* HELLO.

grey huīsède [hway-ser-der]

ground dìshang [dee-shahng]

ground floor yīcéng [yee-tsung]

GROUND FLOOR
Note that the Chinese system of counting floors parallels the American one, that is to say our 'ground floor' is their 'first floor' and our 'first floor' is their 'second floor' etc.

guarantee (*noun*) bǎozhèng [bow-jung]
(*certificate*) bǎoxiūdān [bow-syoh-dahn]

there's a one-year guarantee bǎo xiū yìnián [bow syoh yee-nyen]

guest kèren [ker-run]

GUESTS

Unless you already have friends in China it is unlikely that you will stay with a family (but *see* HOME).

As a guest in China, one of the first things you will discover is that your hosts will go to enormous lengths to insulate you from the realities of life in China. They will assume that you want the best accommodation and transport, and you will find it quite difficult to see anything of the way the majority of the population lives. If that is what you want, gentle persistence is likely to be more effective than blunt insistence. It is quite likely that your hosts will have only limited authority and insisting on something that they simply do not have the power to deliver is guaranteed to cause maximum embarrassment. The converse of this is that, if you make it clear that you are willing to fit in with the local way of doing things, people will often go out of their way to accommodate you.

guidebook yóulǎn shǒucè [yoh-lahn shoh-tser]

H

hair tóufa [toh-fah]
haircut lǐfà [lee-fah]
hairdresser's lǐfà diàn [lee-fah dyen]

HAIRDRESSERS
Hairdressers inside hotels and on the streets also provide a head and shoulders massage. In some back streets, barbers set up their chair on any free pavement space providing both a cheap service and entertainment.

half bàn [bahn]
    half each yìrén yíbànr [yee-run yee-bahnr]
    half a kilo bàn gōngjīn [bahn goong-jin]
    half an hour bàn xiǎoshi [bahn syow-shur]
    See TIME TELLING.

hand shǒu [shoh]

HAND : HOLDING HANDS
Holding hands in public with members of the opposite sex was stopped during the Cultural Revolution and, in comparison with the West, is something that is rarely seen. In contrast adults of the same sex may well hold hands or link arms while walking along, without this carrying any suggestion of homosexuality.

hand baggage shǒutí xíngli [shoh-tee sying-lee]
handbag nǚyòng shǒutíbāo [nyew-yoong shoh-tee-bow]
handkerchief shǒujuànr [shoh-jyew-ahnr]

HANDKERCHIEFS
It is quite common for Chinese to blow their noses directly onto the street using their fingers rather than a handkerchief. Handkerchiefs are used particularly by more sophisticated city-dwellers, but paper tissues are hard to come by.

happy kuàilè [kwI-ler]
    we're not happy with ... ... wǒmen duì ... bù mǎnyì [wor-mun dway ... boo mahn-yee]

hard yìng
    (*difficult*) nán [nahn]

hat màozi [mow-dzur]

have yǒu [yoh]
    can I have ...? nǐ néng bù néng géi wǒ ...? [nee
    nung boo nung gay wor]
    (*literally: you can not can give me?*)
    I don't have ... wǒ méi yǒu ... [wor may yoh]
    do you have ...? ní yǒu méi yǒu ...?
    he has ... tā yǒu ...
    we have ... wǒmen yǒu ... [wor-mun yoh]
    they have ... tāmen yǒu ...
    have they ...? tāmen yǒu méi yǒu ...?
    I have to ... wó děi ... [wor day]
    I have to leave tomorrow wǒ míngtian yídìng déi zǒu
    [wor ming-tyen yee-ding day dzoh]

he tā [tah]

HE

In spoken Chinese the word **tā** can mean both 'he'
and 'she' (but there are different characters for the
two in written Chinese). The same word can also
mean 'him' and 'her' either as a direct or as an
indirect object.

    tā shi lǎoshī
    he/she is a teacher

    tā rènshi wǒ
    he/she knows me

    wǒ rènshi tā
    I know him/her

    tā jì gei wǒ le
    he/she sent it to me

    wǒ jì gei tā le
    I sent it to him/her

head tóu [toh]

headache tóuténg [toh-tung]

health jiànkāng [jyen-kahng]
    your very good health! zhù nǐ jiànkāng! [joo nee jyen-
    kahng]

hear tīngjiàn [ting-jyen]
    I can't hear wǒ tīng bú jiàn [wor ting boo jyen]
    (*literally: I listen not hear*)

heart xīnzàng [syin-dzahng]

heavy zhòng [joong]

heel (*of foot*) jiǎo hòugēn [jyow hoh-gun]
  (*of shoe*) xié hòugēn [syeh hoh-gun]

hello ní hǎo [nee how]
  (*on telephone*) wéi [way]

HELLO

Although there is a fairly standard way of saying
hello in Chinese, which foreigners can use, there is
also quite an interesting diversity of forms of greeting. Here are some examples:

The commonest formal greetings that Westerners
can use are:

> **ní hǎo**
> [nee how]
> hello

to which the response is also:

> **ní hǎo**

You can also say **nín hǎo,** which is a slightly politer
version.

A further inquiry:

> **nǐ shēnti hǎo ma?**
> [nee shun-tee how mah]
> (*literally: you health good (question word)*)

is roughly equivalent to:
  how are you?

and the response is:

> **hén hǎo, nǐ ne?**
> [hun how nee ner]
> fine, and you?

Chinese people do not usually use these with people
they know well or see often, but prefer just to say the
name of the person they have just met. For example,
if a Chinese meets his young friend called Wang, he
will usually say:

> **èi, Xiǎo Wáng**
> [ay syow wahng]
> (*literally: oh, young Wang*)

which is the equivalent of saying hello. He might
also say:

> **nǐ lái le**
> [nee lI ler]
> (*literally: you've come*)

if Wang has come to see him, this again being a way
of saying hello.

When Chinese meet in the street they may greet
each other with:

> **nǐ qù nǎr?**
> [nee chyew nahr]
> (*literally: where are you going*)

This is a polite formula, not necessarily nosiness on
the part of the inquirer. The reply will depend on
where you are going but something like:

> **wǒ jìnchéng**
> [wor jin-chung]
> I am going into town

or: **wǒ chūqu**
> [wor choo-chyew]
> I'm going out

is quite acceptable.

Around meal times people may ask:

> **chīfàn le?**
> [chur-fahn ler]

or: **chī le?**
> [chur ler]

both of which mean literally:

> have you eaten?

To this you can reply:

> **chī le**
> [chur ler]
> (*literally: I have eaten*)

or: **hái méi chī ne**
> [hI may chur ner]
> (*literally: I have not yet eaten*)

both of which are actually ways of returning the
greeting, and not comments on the state of your
stomach.

help (*noun*) bāngzhù [bahng-joo]
  help! jiùmìng a! [jyoh-ming ah]
  I need somebody to help me wǒ xūyào yǒurén
  bāngmáng [wor syew-yow yoh-run bahng-mahng]

her (*possessive adjective*) tāde [tah-der]
  (*pronoun*) tā
  See HIS.

here zhèr [jer]

hers tāde [tah-der]
  See HIS.

high (*hill, costs*) gāo [gow]

hill shān [shahn]

him tā [tah]
  See HE.

hire chūzū [choo-dzoo]
  I want to hire a car wó xiǎng zū liàng chē [wor syahng dzoo lyahng cher]
  There is no self-drive car hiring in China. This phrase literally means 'I want to hire a taxi'.

his tāde [tah-der]

HIS
The word for 'his' is formed by adding the particle **de** to the word for he or **tā**. **Tāde** can be used to mean both 'his' as a possessive adjective (as in 'his passport') and 'his' as a possessive pronoun (as in 'it's his'). It can also mean 'her' or 'hers'. For example:

> **tāde hùzhào**
> his (her) passport
>
> **shi tāde**
> it's his (hers)

hole dòng [doong]

holiday (*vacation, public*) jiàxī [jyah-syee]
  (*festival, public holiday*) jiérì [jyeh-rur]
  See PUBLIC HOLIDAYS.

home jiā [jyah]
  at home zài jiā [dzI jyah]
  the home market guónèi shìchǎng [gwor-nay shur-chahng]

HOME
Unless you have friends in China or stay long enough to make friends, it is unlikely that you will be invited to people's homes. Meetings will be in the office of the organization you are visiting or in your hotel, and entertaining is almost always done in a restaurant. Invitations to homes are rare because of a sense of privacy, feelings that too close contact with foreigners might lead to political criticism later and possibly feelings of inadequacy, as Chinese homes are usually far more poorly equipped than Western homes.

City-dwellers tend to live in flats or small houses provided by their work unit. These can be quite cramped, particularly if grandparents are living with

a married couple and their children. Traditional
three-side houses around a courtyard provide more
room but nowadays these are often shared between
several families.

In the countryside, where there is more available
land, and in the wealthier areas in towns, houses are
being rebuilt and extended at an astonishing rate,
with red brick often being used to replace the older
stone construction. Some rural areas are offering
home-stay to tourists (after the Japanese pattern)
which enables visitors to spend a few nights in
traditional farm homes. This is still at the experi-
mental stage, so it would be best to inquire at China
Travel. You might say:

> **wǒ kéyi dào Zhōngguo ren de jiāli zhù ma?**
> [wor ker-yee dow joong-gwor run der jyah-lee joo
> mah]
> could I stay in a Chinese home?

Some northern rural houses are effectively caves, as
they are built into the hills for warmth and solidity.
This is very common in the north-west, particularly
in Shaanxi province.

Hong Kong Xiānggǎng [syang-gahng]

hope: I hope so wǒ xīwàng shi zhèiyàng [wor syee-
wahng shur jay-yahng]
I hope not wǒ xīwàng bú shi zhèiyàng

horrible zāotòule [dzow-toh-ler]

hospital yīyuàn [yee-yew-ahn]

hospitality hàokè [how-ker]
thank you for your hospitality xièxie nínde
shèngqíng kuǎndài [syeh-syeh neen-der shung-ching
kwahn-dI]

HOSPITALITY

Much Chinese hospitality for foreign visitors is
formalized, although the welcome and enjoyment is
not necessarily less genuine because of this. Official
visitors or delegations can expect to be taken out to a
restaurant by the organization responsible for them,
and if you have stayed a long time or have been
given particularly helpful treatment a reciprocal
invitation will be appreciated.

Banquets or restaurant meals tend to start much
earlier than in the West, perhaps as early as 6.30 in
the evening. They may last between an hour and a
half and two hours, but they are unlikely to continue

until late at night. Punctuality is very important. Small talk – **kèqihuà** – always precedes and accompanies the meal and even the most sumptuous banquet will be preceded by apologies for the poor quality of the food!

host zhǔrén [joo-run]
See GUESTS.

hot rè [rer]
(*spicy*) là [lah]

HOTELS
China has a variety of different types of hotel and a variety of different words to describe them.

The main types of hotel which cater for foreigners as well as for Chinese senior government officials and party officials are called:

fàndiàn　饭店
[fahn-dyen]

They are also known as:

bīnguǎn
[bin-gwahn]
guest house

The smaller and cheaper types of hotel which are primarily used by Chinese travellers are called:

lǚguǎn
[lyew-gwahn]

Foreigners touring China on a shoestring have used these, although the authorities do not approve and will try to direct you to pricier hotels. You should be warned that facilities are quite basic and several people usually share a room. So you might well find yourself sharing with complete strangers – either foreigners or Chinese. Most of them will provide only a bed and no meals. Large numbers of these **lǚguǎn** have sprung up recently to cope with the enormous increase in the quantity of Chinese touring their own country.

In some parts of China, the word **fàndiàn** means a restaurant (its literal meaning being 'food shop') and cheap hotels are known as **lǚshè**.
See also JOINT VENTURE HOTELS.

hour xiǎoshi [syow-shur]
(*literally: small time*)

in an hour yíge xiǎoshi yǐhòu [yee-ger syow-shur yee-hoh]
See TIME TELLING.

house fángzi [fahng-dzur]
See HOME.

how zěnme [dzun-mah]
    how do I get to ...? dào ... zěnme zǒu? [dow ... dzun-mah dzoh]
    how do you do? ní hǎo [nee how]
    how long? yào duō jiǔ? [yow dwor jyoh]
    how long does it take? (*journey etc.*) yào duō cháng shíjian? [yow dwor chahng shur-jyen]
    how many? duōshǎo? [dwor-show]
    (*if the answer is likely to be ten or less*) jǐge? [jee-ger]
    how much? duōshǎo? [dwor-show]
    (*cost*) duōshǎo qián? [dwor-show chyen]

humour yōumò [yoh-mor]

HUMOUR

Although jokes do not translate very well, Chinese humour is basically the same as any other. It is very important to realize that dirty jokes or innuendoes will not go down well and are not regarded as an essential way of establishing rapport. Anything that is likely to impair someone's dignity should be avoided. Jokes about personal and political matters can easily cause offence.

If you look at Chinese cartoons you will see that they rely for their effect on satire or gently poking fun rather than on a punchline or strong visual humour. The most subtle and typically Chinese forms of humour like the cross-talk dialogue – **xiàngsheng** – and the clowns in Peking Opera – **Jīngjù** – are only really accessible if you learn to speak and understand Chinese.

hungry è [er]
    I'm hungry wǒ èle [wor er-ler]
    I'm not very hungry wǒ bù zěnme è [wor boo dzun-mah er]

hurry: hurry! kuài diǎnr! [kwI dyenr]
    there's no hurry mànman lái [mahn-mahn lI]
    (*literally: slow slow come*)

hurt: it hurts téng [tung]
    it doesn't hurt bù téng

husband zhàngfu [jahng-foo]

HUSBANDS

The formal word for husband is **zhàngfu** but in the
People's Republic the word:

àiren
[I-run]

is preferred. It means 'spouse' so can be used for
either husband or wife. A word of warning, though:
avoid using **àiren** with Standard Chinese speakers
from Taiwan or Hong Kong, where it means 'lover'.

I

I wǒ [wor]

I

In spoken Chinese the word **wǒ** can mean both 'I' and 'me'. It remains the same whether used as a direct or indirect object.

> **wǒ shi Yīngguo ren**
> [wor shur ying-gwor run]
> I am English

> **wǒ bú rènshi tā**
> [wor boo run-shur tah]
> I don't know him

> **tā bú rènshi wǒ**
> he doesn't know me

> **wǒ jì gei tā le**
> [wor jee gay tah ler]
> I sent it to him

> **tā jì gei wǒ le**
> he sent it to me

ice bīng
  with ice jiā bīngkuàir [jyah bing-kwI-r]

ice cream bīngjilíng [bing-jee-ling]

if rúguǒ [roo-gwor]

ill yǒu bìng [yoh bing]
  I feel ill wǒ juéde bù shūfu [wor jyew-eh-der boo shoo-foo]

immediately mǎshang [mah-shahng]

IMPERATIVES

It is possible to make a simple imperative in Chinese using just the verb, with or without a pronoun, and using a commanding tone of voice:

> **guò lái!**
> come here!

> **nǐ zuò zhèr!**
> sit here!

But Chinese tends to avoid direct orders – requests and suggestions are more common. Two ways of forming polite imperatives in Chinese are: using the word **qǐng**, which means 'please', or putting the word **ba** (a particle used to indicate suggestions) at the end of a sentence. For example:

> **qǐng jìnlai**
> [ching jin-lI]
> please come in

> **wǒmen zǒu ba**
> [wor-mun dzoh bah]
> let's go

> **zài chī diǎnr ba**
> [dzI chur dyen-r bah]
> eat a bit more

To form the negative, to say 'don't do . . .' the most useful wor is **bié**. For example:

> **qǐng ni bié zhàoxiàng**
> [ching nee byeh jow-syahng]
> please don't take photographs

> **bié zǒu le**
> [byeh dzoh ler]
> don't go

> **bié wàng le**
> [byeh wahng ler]
> don't forget

You can also use the word **búyào** (*literally: don't want to*) instead of **bié**. For example:

> **búyào gàosu tā**
> [boo-yow gow-soo tah]
> don't tell her

> **búyào jìnqu**
> [boo-yow jin-chyew]
> don't go in

> **qǐng ni búyào zhàoxiàng**
> [ching nee boo-yow jow-syahng]
> please don't take photographs

import (*verb*) jìnkǒu [jin-koh]

important zhòngyao [joong-yow]
  it is very important hěn zhòngyao [hun joong-yow]

impossible bù kěnéng [boo ker-nung]

in zai . . . li [dzI . . . lee]
  in China zai Zhōngguó [dzI joong-gwor]
  in Chinese (*literally: using Chinese*) yòng Hànyǔ
  [yoong hahn-yew]

in my room zai wǒde fángjiān li [dzI wor-der fahng-jyen lee]

in two weeks from now liǎngge xīngqī yǐhòu [lyahng-ger sying-chee yee-hoh]

IN

The word **zài** (which is not stressed in a sentence) on its own indicates that you are going to say something about the location of the noun that follows. Where it is perfectly clear what is meant, as in:

zai Běijīng
in Beijing

zai Zhōngguó
in China

Zài can be used on its own. However, **zài** can also be used with words like **shang** – on, **xiàtou** – under and **wàitou** – outside. Where there is possible ambiguity you use **zai . . . li** or **zai . . . lǐmianr** to mean 'in':

zai wǒde fángjiān li
in my room

zai hézi lǐmianr
in/inside the box

included: is . . . included? . . . bāokuò zàinèi ma? [bow-kwor dzI-nay mah]

India Yìndu [yin-doo]

Indian (*adjective*) Yìndu
(*person*) Yìndu ren [yin-doo run]

industry gōngyè [goong-yeh]

inflation (*economics*) tōnghuò péngzhàng [toong-hwor pung-jahng]

information xiāoxi [syow-syee]

information desk wènxùnchù [wun-syewn-choo]

instant coffee sùróng kāfēi [soo-roong kah-fay]

insurance báoxiǎn [bow-syen]

interesting yǒu yìsi [yoh yee-sur]
  that's very interesting zhēn yǒu yìsi [jun yoh yee-sur]

international guójì [gwor-jee]

international driving licence guójí tōngyòng jiàshǐ zhízhào [gwor-jee toong-yoong jyah-shur jur-jow]

interpret fānyì [fahn-yee]
  could you please interpret? qíng nǐ fānyì yíxia, hǎo ma? [ching nee fahn-yee yee-syah how mah]

interpreter fānyì [fahn-yee]
   we need an interpreter wŏmen xūyào yíwèi fānyì
   [wor-mun syew-yow yee-way fahn-yee]

introduce jièshao [jyeh-show]
   may I introduce ...? wŏ lái jièshao yíxia – zhèiwei
   shi ... [wor ll jyeh-show yee-syah – jay-way shur]
   (*literally: let me introduce – this is ...*)

INTRODUCTIONS

Introductions are informal and straightforward and
carried out in a way similar to what we are
accustomed to. The person doing the introducing
would say:

   wŏ lái jièshao yíxia
   [wor ll jyeh-show yee-syah]
   let me introduce you

and then for example:

   zhèiwei shi Zhāng Xiānsheng
   [jay-way shur jahng syen-shung]
   this is Mr Zhang

To introduce a third person to the person you are
with, you use exactly the same phrase:

   wŏ lái jièshao yíxia – zhèiwei shi Màikèmĭlán
   Xiānsheng
   [wor ll jyeh-show yee-syah – jay-way shur
   Macmillan syen-shung]
   let me introduce Mr Macmillan
   (*literally: let me introduce – this is Mr Macmillan*)

To introduce yourself, you can just say:

   wŏ xìng ...
   [wor sying]

and give your surname.

  Business cards are becoming more common in
China although there is nothing like the ritual
associated with them in Japan. Western visitors who
take the trouble to have a Chinese translation of
their name and position printed on the reverse side
of the card will find it greatly appreciated.

invitation yāoqĭng [yow-ching]
   thank you for the invitation xièxie nínde yāoqĭng
   [syeh-syeh neen-der yow-ching]

INVITATIONS

The foreign visitor to China on official or commercial business will always be invited out for a meal by
the host organization. It is not necessary for an

individual to reciprocate, but with a large group of visitors or where the stay is a prolonged one, this would be appreciated. *See* GUESTS, HOSPITALITY.

invite yāoqǐng [yow-ching]
    can I invite you out for a meal? wǒ kéyi qǐng nǐ chūqu chīfàn ma? [wor ker-yee ching nee choo-chyew chur-fahn mah]

invoice (*noun*) zhàngdānr [jahng-dahn-r]

INVOICES
In China it is normal to pay first and receive the goods later, so an invoice is a rarity. But as China opens up more and more to international trade, accepted international business practices are becoming more widespread, at least in business relations between Chinese and foreign organizations. They are trickling through more slowly to business relations between Chinese. Financing of trade with China is a complex business and the situation is changing constantly. Consult your Chinese embassy for details.

Ireland Ài'ěrlán [I-er-lahn]

Irish Ài'ěrlán [I-er-lahn]
    I'm Irish wǒ shi Ài'ěrlán ren [wor shur I-er-lahn run]

iron (*for clothes*) yùndǒu [yewn-doh]
    (*material*) tiě [tyeh]
    could you please get these ironed? qǐng bāng wǒ yùnyun zhèixie yīfu, hǎo ma? [ching bahng wor yewn-yewn jay-syeh yee-foo how mah]

is shì [shur]; *see* BE

island dǎo [dow]

it: it is . . . shi . . . [shur]
    is it . . .? shi . . . ma?
It is possible to use **tā** for 'it' but the word is rarely used in spoken Chinese. The context makes the meaning clear. For example:
    it's me
    shi wǒ
    (*literally: is me*)
    is it far?
    yuǎn ma?
    (*literally: far?*)

is it ready?
hăole ma?
(*literally: ready?*)

can I try it?
wo néng shìshi ma?
(*literally: I can try?*)

it is a good hotel
shi ge hăo fàndiàn
(*literally: is a good hotel*)

J

jacket shàngyī [shahng-yee]
See CLOTHES.

jade yù [yew]

jam (*for bread*) guǒjiàng [gwor-jyahng]

January yīyue [yee-yew-eh]

Japan Rìben [rer-bun]

Japanese (*adjective*) Rìben [rer-bun]
(*person*) Rìben ren [rer-bun run]
(*language*) Rìyǔ [rer-yew]

jetlag: I'm/he's suffering from jetlag wǒ/tā zuò fēijī zuòde bíjiào lèi [wor/tah dzwor fay-jee dzwor-der bee-jyow lay]

jewellery shǒushi [shoh-shur]

job (*work*) gōngzuò [goong-dzwor]
what's your job? nǐ shi zuò shénme gōngzuò de? [nee shur dzwor shun-mah goong-dzwor der]
tender for a job tóubiāo [toh-byow]
if we get this job rúguǒ wǒmende tóubiāo chénggōng de huà [roo-gwor wor-mun-der toh-byow chung-goong der hwah]

Joint Venture hézī jīngyíng qǐyè [her-dzur jing-ying chee-yeh]

Joint Venture hotel hézī jīngyíng de fàndiàn [her-dzur jing-ying der fahn-dyen]

JOINT VENTURE HOTELS
The most prestigious and modern hotels in China have been built by joint Chinese and foreign investment. They include the Great Wall Hotel in Beijing and the White Swan in Guangzhou. These are the largest and most expensive in China and aim at the international standards of hotels in Europe, the USA and Japan. They cater especially for business people and their prices put them out of range of the budget traveller and the vast majority of Chinese. Their restaurants are usually open to non-residents and Western newspapers are available.

joke (*noun*) wánxiào [wahn-syow]
  you're joking! nǐ zài kāi wánxiào ba! [nee dzI kI
  wahn-syow bah]

journey lǚxíng [lyew-sying]
  safe journey! yílù píng'ān! [yee-loo ping-ahn]

July qīyue [chee-yew-eh]

June liùyue [lyoh-yew-eh]

just (*only*) zhǐ [jur]
  I just want one wó zhǐ yào yíge [wor jur yow yee-ger]
  I'll have just a little bit wó zhǐ yào yìdiǎnr [wor jur
  yow yee-dyen-r]

K

keep: please keep it qǐng názhe ba [ching nah-jer bah]
  keep the change búyòng zhǎo le [boo-yoong jow ler]

key yàoshi [yow-shur]
  the key for room number ... ... hào fángjiān de
  yàoshi [how fahng-jyen der yow-shur]

kilo gōngjīn [goong-jin]

kilometre gōngli [goong-lee]

kind: that's very kind of you nǐ zhēn hǎo [nee jun how]
  what kind of ...? shénme yàngr de ...? [shun-mah
  yahng-r der]

kiss (*noun*) wěn [wun]

KISSING

Adult Chinese simply do not kiss in public and
youngsters do so only rarely. An American teacher
recounted with obvious enjoyment the expressions
on the faces of her husband's Chinese colleagues as
she kissed him goodbye at Hefei airport. Social
kissing is likely to be misinterpreted, so don't do it!

kitchen chúfáng [choo-fahng]

knee xīgài [syee-gI]

knife dāozi [dow-dzur]
  can I have a knife and fork, please? qǐng géi wǒ yífù
  dāochā, hǎo ma? [ching gay wor yee-foo dow-chah
  how mah]

know (*a fact*) zhīdao [jur-dow]
  (*a person*) rènshi [run-shur]
  I don't know wǒ bù zhīdao [wor boo jur-dow]
  I know him wǒ rènshi tā
  I don't know him wǒ bú rènshi tā
  I didn't know that nà wǒ bù zhīdao
  do you know where ... is? nǐ zhīdao ... zai nǎr ma?
  [nee jur-dow ... dzI nahr mah]
  I knew him wǒ rènshi tā
You will see that the Chinese for 'I knew him' is
exactly the same as the Chinese for 'I know him'.
The Chinese language allows context to determine
whether a speaker is talking about the present or

about the past. If you like, you can use an extra phrase to pinpoint the time you are talking about, for example:

I knew him at school
wǒ shàngxué de shíhou rènshi tā

But you will see that the verb is still unchanged; the phrase 'at school' determines past reference. *See* PAST TENSE.

Korea: North Korea Běi Cháoxiǎn [bay chow-syen]
South Korea Nán Cháoxiǎn [nahn chow-syen]

Korean (*adjective*) Cháoxiǎn [chow-syen]
(*person*) Cháoxiǎn ren [chow-syen run]

L

ladies (*toilet*) nǚ cèsuǒ [nyew tser-swor]

lady nǚshi [nyew-shur]

lake hú [hoo]

lamb (*animal*) yánggāo [yahng-gow]
(*meat*) yángròu [yahng-roh]

lane (*narrow street*) hútòng [hoo-toong]
The **hútòng** refers to the crowded back streets of
Beijing and some other cities, meaning both the
lanes themselves and the houses off them.

language yǔyán [yew-yen]

Laos Lǎowō [low-wor]

large dà [dah]

last (*last in series*) zuìhòu [dzway-hoh]
(*latest*) zuìjìn [dzway-jin]
last week shàng(ge) xīngqī [shahng-ger sying-chee]
last night zuótian wǎnshang [dzwor-tyen wahn-
shahng]
last year qùnián [chyew-nyen]
the last time we met wǒmen shàngci jiànmiàn de
shíhou [wor-mun shahng-tsur jyen-myen der shur-
hoh]
last but not least zuìhòu [dzway-hoh]

late wǎn [wahn]
sorry for being late duìbuqǐ, wǒ lái wǎnle [dway-boo-
chee wor ll wahn-ler]
delivery will be two weeks late jiāohuò huì yǒu
liǎngge xīngqī de dāngē [jyow-hwor hway yoh
lyahng-ger sying-chee der dahn-ger]

later guò yìhuǐr [gwor yee-hway-r]
I'll come back later wǒ guò yìhuǐr huílai [wor gwor
yee-hway-r hway-ll]
You use **guò yìhuǐr** when the delay is only relatively
short. If you are referring to something that is going
to happen much later then the word **yǐhòu**, which
also means 'afterwards', must be used.

laugh (*verb*) xiào [syow]

LAUGHING

Chinese people laugh at jokes, cartoons and minor indignities like people slipping in the street just like anyone else, but a laugh may also indicate that you have embarrassed someone by raising a taboo subject or by asking to do something that it is not in their power to arrange. *See also* EMBARRASSMENT.

laundry xǐyidiàn [syee-yee-dyen]

law fǎlǜ [fah-lyew]

lawyer lǜshī [lyew-shur]

learn xuéxí [syew-eh-syee]
  I'd like to learn Chinese wǒ xiǎng xuéxí Hànyǔ [wor syahng syew-eh-syee hahn-yew]

leave (*depart*) zǒu [dzoh]
  I'm leaving in the morning wǒ shàngwu zǒu [wor shahng-woo dzoh]
  when does the plane leave? fēijī jídiǎn qǐfēi? [fay-jee jee-dyen chee-fay]
  when does the train leave? huǒchē jídiǎn kāi? [hwor-chur jee-dyen kI]

left zuǒbiānr [dzwor-byenr]
  on the left zai zuǒbiānr [dzI dzwor-byenr]

left luggage (office) xíngli jìcúnchù [sying-lee jee-tsoon-choo]

leg tuǐ [tway]

less shǎo [show]
  less than a year búdào yìnián [boo-dow yee-nyen]

letter (*mail*) xìn [syin]

letter of credit xìnyòng zhèng [syin-yoong jung]

letterbox xìnxiāng [syin-syahng]　信箱

LETTERS

Letters to businessmen or organizations should be in Chinese or have a Chinese translation if possible. Otherwise a standard typed letter in English will be easiest for the organization to translate. *See also* ADDRESSES.

If you are writing to an individual in China, you should get their permission to do so first, especially for personal letters. In the past, many Chinese have been in serious trouble with the authorities for having private contacts with foreigners and, although the atmosphere is much more relaxed at present, some people are still cautious, particularly if they are in a politically or scientifically sensitive job. If anyone does give you an address to write to then you can assume that they are able to correspond with you.

Correspondence in general is likely to be more sporadic than in the West and routine acknowledgement of a letter is by no means a standard procedure. Lack of a reply does not necessarily mean a refusal or a snub. It is often necessary to write several letters before an answer is received, so if an urgent reply is vital, you should make this clear and ask your correspondent to reply by a certain date.

Christmas and New Year cards are not sent by many Chinese although the practice is beginning to spread. Cards from foreigners are likely to be appreciated.

lift (*elevator*) diàntī [dyen-tee]

light (*electric*) diàndēng [dyen-dung]
  (*not dark*) míngliàng [ming-lyahng]
  (*not heavy*) qīng [ching]
  do you have a light? ní yóu huǒchái ma? [nee yoh hwor-chI mah]
  the light's not working dēng bú liàng [dung boo lyahng]

like: I'd like a . . . wó xiǎng . . . [wor syahng]
  would you like a . . .? ní xiǎng bu xiǎng . . .?
  (*literally: you like not like*)
  I like it wó xǐhuan [wor syee-hwahn]
  I don't like it wǒ bù xǐhuan
  he likes it tā xǐhuan
  he doesn't like it tā bù xǐhuan
  like this gēn zhèige yíyàng [gun jay-ger yee-yahng]

litre shēng [shung]

little (*small*) xiǎo [syow]
  a little yìdiǎnr [yee-dyen-r]
  a little sugar yìdiǎnr táng

live zhù [joo]
  I live in . . . wǒ zhù zai . . . [wor joo dzI]

LOAN WORDS

There are very few loan words from Western languages in standard Chinese and the contrast with Japanese, where there are thousands, is quite remarkable. The usual way of incorporating a Western technical term or concept is to translate the idea rather than just adapt a foreign word. Before the war, the word **tiělèfēng** was sometimes used for 'telephone', but this has disappeared completely and the universal word is now **diànhuà**, which literally means 'electric speech'. Many words from the vocabulary of science or social science have come into Chinese through Japanese since the nineteenth century. These were written in **kanji** (Japanese Chinese characters) and formed according to Chinese principles and are now completely indistinguishable from native Chinese words.

Chinese dialects have incorporated some loan words from English, particularly the Cantonese dialect which has a link with the English-speaking world in Hong Kong. The two most common examples of this are **dīk-si** (taxi) and **bā-si** (bus).

Loan words in standard Chinese include:

> **āsīpīlín**
> [ah-sur-pee-lin]
> aspirin

> **qiǎokelì**
> [chow-ker-lee]
> chocolate

> **pánníxīlín**
> [pan-nee-syee-lin]

sometimes used colloquially for penicillin, although

> **qīngméisù**
> [ching-may-soo]

is the preferred scientific term.

> **xiāngbīnjiǔ**
> [syahng-bin-joh]
> champagne

lock (*on door*) suǒ [swor]
    it's locked suǒ shang le [swor shahng ler]
    excuse me, I'm locked out duìbuqǐ, wó bǎ zìji suǒzai wàibiānr le [dway-boo-chee wor bah dzur-jee swor-dzI wI-byen-r ler]

London Lúndūn [loon-doon]

long cháng [chahng]
    a long time hěn cháng shíjian [hun chahng shur-jyen]

look: can I have a look? kànkan kéyi ma? [kahn-kahn ker-yee mah]
    I'm just looking, thanks wó zhǐ shi kànyikàn, xièxie [wor jur shur kahn-yee-kahn syeh-syeh]

that looks good nà kàngshangqu búcuò [nah kahn-shahng-chew boo-tswor]

I look forward to meeting you again xīwàng hái you jīhuì zàici jiàndao nǐ [syee-wahng hI yoh jee-hway dzI-tsur jyen-dow nee]

lorry kǎchē [kah-cher]

lose diū [dyoh]
　I've lost my ... wǒde ... diūle [wor-der ... dyoh-ler]
　I'm lost, can you help me? wǒ míle lù, nǐ néng bāngzhù wǒ ma? [wor mee-ler loo nee nung bahng-joo wor mah]

lot: a lot of ... hěnduō ... [hun-dwor]
　a lot hěnduō
　a lot better hǎoduō le [how-dwor ler]
　not a lot bù duō
　do you see him a lot? – no, not a lot nǐ cháng jiàn tā ma? – bù cháng jiàn [nee chahng jyen tah mah – boo chahng jyen]

Note the Chinese way of saying 'no, not a lot' here: the verb used in the question asked is repeated in the answer in combination with the negative word **bù**. The Chinese means literally:

　　question: you see him a lot (question word)?
　　answer: not lot see

love (*noun*) liàn'ài [lyen'I]
　I love you wǒ ài nǐ [wor I nee]

lovely hǎo [how]
　(*stay*) yúkuài [yew-kwI]

low (*not high*) dī [dee]
　(*prices*) piányide

luck: good luck! zhù nǐ shùnlì! [joo nee shoon-lee]

luggage xíngli [sying-lee]
　my luggage wǒde xíngli [wor-der sying lee]

lunch wǔfàn [woo-fahn]

LUNCH

China tends to take long lunch breaks of up to two hours, starting between eleven and twelve. In the hot south during the summer months lunch breaks can be up to three hours long. Lunch for city people is eaten in the works or office canteen and is followed by a siesta or **xiūxi** [syoh-syee]. Well-organized people have camp-beds in the office, but otherwise you can just stretch out on your desk. Visitors will be encouraged to **xiūxi** (rest) during the lunch break partly out of polite consideration and partly so that they do not disrupt their hosts' siesta.

Many museums and tourist sites may also be closed for up to three hours from 11.30 or 12 onwards.

M

machine jīqì [jee-chee]

mad fēng [fung]
    he must be mad tā yídìng fēngle [tah yee-ding fung-ler]

mail (*noun: letters*) yóujiàn [yoh-jyen]
    (*verb*) jì [jee]
    we'll mail it wǒmen bǎ tā jì zǒu [wor-mun bah tah jee dzoh]

make zhìzào [jur-dzow]
    our company make these (products) wǒmen gōngsi zhìzào zhèixie (chánpǐn) [wor-mun goong-sur jur-dzow jay-syeh (chahn-pin)]

man nánde [nahn-der]
    the men who ... ... de (nèixie) rén [der (nay-syeh) run]

management: our management (*people*) wǒmende guánlǐ rényuán [wor-mun-der gwahn-lee run-yew-ahn]
    your management nǐmende guánlǐ rényuán

manager (*of restaurant, hotel, business etc.*) jīnglǐ [jing-lee]

managing director zǒng jīnglǐ [dzoong jing-lee]

Mandarin (*language*) *see* **Standard Chinese**

manners lǐmào [lee-mow]
    good manners yóu lǐmào [yoh lee-mow]
    bad manners méi lǐmào [may lee-mow]

many hěn duō [hun dwor]
    not many taxis méiyou hěn duō chūzūchē [may-yoh hun dwor choo-dzoo-cher]

Mao Tse Tung jacket zhōngshānzhuāng [joong-shahn-jwahng]

map dìtú [dee-too]
    I'd like a map of ... wó xiǎngyào zhāng ... (de) dìtú [wor syahng-yow jahng ... (der) dee-too]

MAPS
Good maps of the provinces open to tourists and the main Chinese cities are now available in English and can be bought in China, and in Britain from map

dealers and specialist Chinese bookshops. They are adequate for the major roads and the main sightseeing attractions, but they are not detailed enough to cover all the side roads or the hutongs (alleyways), of Beijing, for example. A detailed street map of Beijing was published in Chinese in 1982. Maps of country areas with footpaths and small roads for walkers are not available. For many years few maps were published either for Chinese or for visitors. Nowadays in most cities a street map is available which also shows the bus routes – this can be of great help to visitors exploring the town by themselves.

March sānyue [sahn-yew-eh]

market (*also for business*) shìchǎng [shur-chahng]

MARKETS

The Chinese have had a talent for trade for centuries but much of this was suppressed for the first thirty years of the People's Republic. It has now burst forth in the free markets which have appeared in every town and city (as well as in the countryside) challenging the former monopoly of the state-run shops. Vegetables, fruit and other foods are the main wares, but there are also clothes, souvenirs and many other items. They are often far cheaper and more authentically Chinese than the carefully selected stock of the Friendship Stores. You can barter in the markets, but foreigners have been fleeced. Make sure you take some small denomination coins to give the right change.

MARRIAGE

Weddings are civil matters and they are major events, particularly in the wealthier rural areas where parents often spend fortunes on wedding presents and setting up the happy couple in their new home. Elderly country people still depend on their sons, so an expensive wedding is seen as an investment even if it is financially crippling at the time. The presents might include bedding, furniture, a sewing machine or a bicycle and even a hi-fi, with the colour red for good luck being much in evidence. Many young people these days are unhappy about the competitiveness of weddings and dowries and there is a trend towards spending the money on a honeymoon tour of China instead. In the cities, when you get married there is likely to be a collection and presents in the organization you work for. The Marriage Law lays down minimum ages of twenty for men and eighteen for women, but this is still thought to be too young and late marriage is encouraged as a population control measure. Married women keep their maiden names and children take their father's surname, although there are occasionally cases where the mother's surname is used. The demands of work frequently separate couples, sometimes by thousands of miles, and finding a flat or house is a major preoccupation which can take years in the overcrowded cities. There is a common saying that it is harder to find a house than a spouse.

married jiēguòhūn de [jyeh-gwor-hun der]
(*when filling in forms*) yīhūn [yee-hun]
I'm married wǒ chéngjiā le [wor chahng-jyah ler]

martial arts wǔshù [woo-shoo]

marvellous tàibàngle [tI-bahng-ler]

matches huǒchái [hwor-chI]

matter: it doesn't matter méi guānxi [may gwahn-syee]

mattress chuángdiàn [chwahng-dyen]

maximum (*noun*) zuìdà [dzway-dah]

May wǔyue [woo-yew-eh]

may: may I . . .? wǒ kéyi . . . ma? [wor ker-yee mah]
may I have . . .? (*in shop etc.*) wo mǎi . . . [wor mI]
may I have a look? wǒ kéyi kànkan ma? [wor ker-yee kahn-kahn mah]

maybe kěnéng [ker-nung]

me wǒ [wor]
that's for me nà shi (gei) wǒde [nah shur (gay) wor-der]

ME
Wǒ can mean either 'I' or 'me' depending on the context:

> **I told him**
> wǒ gàosu tā le
>
> **he told me**
> tā gàosu wǒ le
>
> **I sent it to him**
> wǒ jì gei tā le

he sent it to me
tā jì gei wǒ le

meal fàn [fahn]
  that was an excellent meal wǒmen chīde hénhǎo
  [wor-mun chur-der hun-how]

MEALS

Breakfast is eaten early, at perhaps 7. Lunch, the main meal of the day for most urban people, comes between 12 and 1, usually in the factory or office canteen. Evening meal times are 5–7 and this is the time that visitors invited to a banquet can expect to be invited to a restaurant. (*See also* BREAKFAST, LUNCH, DINNER.) Many Chinese still take the traditional view that to keep in good health you should eat a good breakfast, fill up at lunchtime and eat little in the evening. In the cities, where most couples work, the evening meal is becoming more important.

mean: what does this character mean? zhèige zì shi shénme yìsi? [jay-ger dzur shur shun-mah yee-sur]

meat ròu [roh]

MEAT

Meat is still relatively expensive and is always served cut in small pieces mixed with the other ingredients of a dish, rather than in large steaks or chops. The most popular meats are pork (**zhūròu** [joo-roh]) and chicken (**jī** [jee]) but beef (**niúròu** [nyoh-roh]) is also eaten and there is a northern taste for mutton (**yángròu** [yahng-roh]). Duck (**yā** [yah]) is also popular, and south of the Yangzi flocks of them can be seen being driven from pond to pond. Duck restaurants in the south sometimes cage them live outside so they can be eaten fresh. Peking duck (**Běijīng kǎoyā** [bay-jing kow-yah]) is probably one of the most famous Chinese meat dishes. Duck has become popular in recent years as it is said to prevent cancer.

medicine yào [yow]

MEDICINE

Both modern Western and traditional Chinese medicine are practised and taught in medical schools. It is assumed that Westerners will want to be treated by doctors trained in Western medicine, but acupuncture, moxibustion (the application of a burning material close to the skin to draw out impurities and sickness) and herbal remedies can be given and are widely used by Chinese.

meet: pleased to meet you jiàndao nín hěn gāoxìng [jyen-dow neen hun gow-sying]

meeting huì(yì) [hway(yee)]
shall we arrange another meeting? wŏmen yào bu yào zài tán yícì? [wor-mun yow boo yow dzI tahn yi-tsur]

MEETING PEOPLE
Business visitors are normally met at the airport or railway station and an interpreter will usually be on hand. After the greetings and introductions, certain formal phrases are usual. The host may well say:

yí lùshang xīnkŭ le
you must have had a tiring journey

to which you can reply:

hái hăo, hái hăo
[hI how hI how]
no, I'm fine

mention: don't mention it (*after someone has said thank you*) búyòng xiè [boo-yoong syeh] (*literally: no need thank*)

menu càidānr [tsI-dahn-r]
the menu, please qĭng ná càidānr lái, hăo ma? [ching nah tsI-dahn-r lI how mah]
See FOOD.

message xìnr [syinr]
can I leave a message? wŏ néng liú ge huà ma? [wor nung lyoh ger hwah mah]
can I leave a message for . . . ? wŏ néng gěi . . . liú ge huà ma? [wor nung gay . . . lyoh ger hwah mah]

metre mĭ [mee]
middle zhōngjiān [joong-jyen]
midnight bànyè [bahn-yeh]
mile yīnglĭ [ying-lee]

MILE
The standard system for measuring distances in China is the metric one. The traditional Chinese system is based on the lĭ, which is roughly half a kilometre.

milk năi [nI]

MILK

Chinese people do not generally like milk and it is said they have difficulty digesting it. Chinese tea is always drunk without milk. Fresh milk is usually available only for babies and the elderly, but some dairy products such as yoghurt and ice cream are widely available in big cities. Milk in cafés is likely to be powdered. However, Mongolians and Tibetans are great consumers of milk and tea with milk or butter in it. In Mongolia alcoholic drinks are made from fermented mare's milk. Hotels for foreign visitors also supply milk.

mine wŏde [wor-der]

MINE

Wŏde also means 'my' when used before a noun:

this is mine
zhèi shi wŏde
[jay shur wor-der]
mine is the new one
wŏde shi xīnde
[wor-der shur syin-der]
my map
wŏde dìtú
[wor-der dee-too]

mineral water kuàngquánshuĭr [kwahng-chew-ahn-shway-r]

Ming tombs Shísān líng [shur-sahn ling]

minimum (*noun*) zuìxiăo [dzway-syow]

minute fēn(zhōng) [fun-joong]
just a minute jiù yìhuĭr [jyoh yee-hway-r]

mirror jìngzi [jing-dzur]

Miss xiáojiĕ [syow-jyeh]
Miss! (*to waitress etc.*) fúwùyuán! [foo-woo-yew-ahn]

MISS

Xiáojiĕ is not very popular in China as it has undesirable bourgeois connotations. To play safe it is better to refer to and call a waitress **fúwùyuán** or **fúwùyuán tóngzhì**.

Fúwùyuán simply means 'service staff' and

tóngzhì [toong-jur], 'comrade', added afterwards makes it politer (*see also* ADDRESSING PEOPLE).

mistake cuò(wu) [tswor(woo)]

MISTAKES

Chinese people may often appear unwilling to admit to a mistake. This may be because they do not care to take personal responsibility for a decision made or for action taken.

modern xiàndài [syen-dI]

Monday xīngqiyī [sying-chee-yee]

money qián [chyen]

MONEY

Chinese currency is the **Rénmínbì** [run-min-bee] (People's Currency) and the unit is the **yuán** [yew-ahn]. This is divided into 100 **fēn** [fun]; ten **fēn** are known as a **jiǎo** [jyow]. These are the words used on notes and coins and in writing about money. But of these words only **fēn** is used in speech. A **yuán** is always called a **kuài** [kwI] (*literally: a piece*) and a **jiǎo** is called a **máo** [mow].

To summarize:

| written: | 1 yuán | 元 | yuán |
| spoken: | 1 kuài | | |

equals:

| written: | 10 jiǎo | 角 | jiǎo |
| spoken: | 10 máo | | |

or:

| written: | 100 fēn | 分 | fēn |
| spoken: | 100 fēn | | |

So for example:

written	spoken
15 fen	1 mao 5
80 fen	8 mao

Coins of 1, 2 and 5 **fēn** are used. For higher values only notes are in circulation.

Some useful phrases in connection with money are:

how much is it?
duōshǎo qián?
[dwor-show chyen]

that's very expensive
zhēn guì
[jun gway]

can you change this into smaller money?
néng bù néng bāng wǒ huàn diǎnr líng de?
[nung boo nung bahng wor hwahn dyen-r ling der]

it cost me . . .
zhèi huāle wǒ . . .
[jay hwah-ler wor]

There is a tendency, when using single units, to add the word **qián**:

liǎng kuài qián
[lyahng kwI chyen]
two kuai
(*literally: two kuai money*)

Chinese money was given a facelift in April 1987 with the introduction of a new series of notes. Notes of denominations over 10 **yuán** have been printed for the first time ever, an indication of growing commercialization and inflation.

Existing notes remain in circulation and the new notes are being introduced gradually starting with the 50 **yuán** or **kuài** and 5 **jiǎo** or **máo**.

The new notes are:

1 yuán	China's Yao and Tong ethnic minorities against the background of the Great Wall
2 yuán	Uygur and Yi people against a south Chinese scenery
5 yuán	Tibetan and Hui people with the Wu gorge on the Yangze River as backdrop
10 yuán	a farmer and portraits of Han Chinese (the ethnic majority) and Mongolians backed by Mount Everest (Qomolangma).
50 yuán	a worker, a farmer and an intellectual set against the Yellow River beauty spot of Hukou
100 yuán	portraits of the late leaders Mao Zedong, Zhou Enlai, Liu Shaoqi and Zhu De

New notes of 1, 2 and 5 **jiǎo** or **máo** are also being issued, but the 1, 2 and 5 **fēn** notes which tend to end up in grubby, crumpled bundles will not be replaced. Coins of 1, 2 and 5 **fēn** will still be in use.
See also FOREIGN EXCHANGE CERTIFICATES.

Mongolia Ménggǔ [mung-goo]

Mongolian (*adjective*) Ménggǔ(de) [mung-goo(der)]
(*noun*) Ménggǔ ren [mung-goo run]

month yue [yew-eh]

MONTHS

The names of months in Chinese are formed by putting a number in front of **yue**, which means month:

January	yīyue	[yee-yew-eh]
February	èryue	[er-yew-eh]
March	sānyue	[sahn-yew-eh]
April	sìyue	[sur-yew-eh]
May	wǔyue	[woo-yew-eh]
June	liùyue	[lyoh-yew-eh]
July	qīyue	[chee-yew-eh]
August	bāyue	[bah-yew-eh]
September	jiǔyue	[jyoh-yew-eh]
October	shíyue	[shur-yew-eh]
November	shíyīyue	[shur-yee-yew-eh]
December	shí'èryue	[shur-er-yew-eh]

To talk about a number of months, you put the classifier **gè** [ger] between the number and **yue**:

> **six months**
> liù ge yue

but: **liùyue**
June

> **eight months**
> bā ge yue

but: **bāyue**
August

> **last month**
> shànggeyue
> [shahng-ger-yew-eh]

> **this month**
> zhèigeyue
> [jay-ger-yew-eh]

> **next month**
> xiàgeyue
> [syah-ger-yew-eh]

moon yuèliang [yew-eh-lyahng]

more gèngduō [gung-dwor]
  no more, thanks bú yàole, xièxie [boo yow-ler syeh-syeh]
  could I have some more? zài lái dianr, hǎo ma? [dzI lI dyen-r how mah]
  more than 100 yìbǎi duō [yee-bI dwor]
  See COMPARISON.

morning zăoshang [dzow-shahng]
   in the morning zăoshang
      tomorrow morning míngtian zăoshang [ming-tyen dzow-shahng]
      this morning jīntian zăoshang [jin-tyen dzow-shahng]
      good morning zăoshang hăo [dzow-shahng how]

mosquito wénzi [wun-dzur]

mosquito net wénzhàng [wun-jahng]

most: most of them tāmen dàduōshù [tah-mun dah-dwor-shoo]

mother mŭqin [moo-chin]

motor mădá [mah-dah]

motorcycle mótuōchē [moh-twoh-cher]

mountain (dà) shān [(dah) shahn]

moustache xiăo húzi [syow hoo-dzur]

mouth zuĭ [dzway]

Mr xiānsheng [syen-shung]

MR
Xiānsheng is not often used between Chinese in the People's Republic but it will be used to Westerners. It also has the slightly quaint meaning of teacher, as a term of respect, like the Japanese **sensei** (*see* ADDRESSING PEOPLE).

Mrs fūren [foo-run]

MRS
Fūren is not often used between Chinese in the People's Republic but it is a polite way of referring to Westerners (*see* ADDRESSING PEOPLE).

Ms nŭshi [nyew-shur]

much: much bigger dà de duō [dah der dwor]
   much faster kuài de duō [kwI der dwor]
      there's not much left méi shèng duōshaole [may shung dwor-show-ler]

music yīnyuè [yin-yew-eh]

MUSIC
Traditional Chinese classical music might sound strange to Western ears at first and a good approach is through the folk song. Anyone who has heard the delightful co-operative efforts of the Chieftains

from Ireland and the Guo brothers from China will realize how close the Celtic and Chinese folk music traditions can sound.

Classical Chinese music uses string and wind instruments not found in the West, the best known being the **píba**, a short lute, and the **èrhú**, a two-stringed violin.

Western visitors can find music at concerts, at the Peking Opera and on radio and television, but the amateurs who sing and play in the parks in the early morning and at street corners at dusk should not be missed.

MUSLIMS

Muslims, **Huí** [hway], are one of the ethnic minorities of China. There may be as many as 35 or 40 million in all, perhaps 20 million living in the cities and the rest in predominantly Muslim areas of the north-west and south-west.

Most city-dwelling Muslims are indistinguishable from the Hàn Chinese in their language or appearance. They do however have special food requirements which are provided for by **Huí** shops, restaurants and snackbars. Some practise Islam and there are mosques in the major cities with large Muslim populations. Chinese Muslims are probably the descendants of Arab and Persian traders who came to China during the seventh and eighth centuries, but they have been almost completely assimilated – except in so far as their religious beliefs are concerned.

The sizeable Muslim community of Níngxià in the north-west has been made into an autonomous region, and Islam is also the religion of the Uighur people of Xīnjiāng province in the far north-west.

must: must I...? wǒ yídìng ... ma? [wor yee-ding mah]
must we...? wǒmen yídìng ... ma? [wor-mun yee-ding mah]
I must... wǒ yídìng ...

my wǒde [wor-der]

MY

Wǒde also means mine when on its own:

    this is my passport
    zhèi shi wǒde hùzhào
    [jay shur wor-der hoo-jow]

this is mine
zhèi shi wŏde
[jay shur wor-der]

When talking about relatives, friends and other things close to you, the **de** can be dropped:

my wife/husband
wŏ àiren
[wor I-run]

my elder brother/younger brother
wŏ gēge/dìdi
[wor ger-ger/dee-dee]

my friend
wŏ péngyou
[wor pung-yoh]

N

nail clippers zhǐjia dāo [jur-jyah dow]

nail scissors xiáo jiǎnzi [syow jyen-dzur]

name míngzi [ming-dzur]
    my name is . . . wǒde míngzi jiào . . . [wor-der ming-dzur jyow]
    what's your name? nǐ jiào shénme míngzi? [nee jyow shun-mah ming-dzur]
    what's his name? tā jiào shénme míngzi?
    what's her name? tā jiào shénme míngzi?
    what's the name of the hotel? zhèijiā fàndiàn jiào shénme? [jay-jyah fahn-dyen jyow shun-mah]

NAMES

The Chinese order for names is first the surname, then the given name, as in Mao Zedong, where Mao is the surname. Li Jianguo would be addressed as Mr Li. But his mother or close friends would call him Jianguo.

Foreign names (including those of the non-Han minorities living in China – *see* NATIONALITY) are transformed into the nearest Chinese phonetic equivalent. Each syllable is allocated a written character which has the same sound. Mrs Thatcher, visiting China, became **Sāqièěr fūren** [sah-chee-er foo-run], and the Queen was known as **Yīlishābái Nüwáng** [yee-lee-shah-bI nyew-wahng] (**Nüwáng** meaning Queen).

Ask a Chinese person to render your name phonetically and to write down the characters, which are always chosen so as to have the best connotations. It is then possible to have a seal (*see* SEALS) carved with your Chinese name. *See also* CHRISTIAN NAMES, SURNAMES, ADDRESSING PEOPLE.

napkin cānjīn [tsahn-jin]
    paper napkin cānjīn zhǐ [tsahn-jin jur]

NAPKINS

Chinese people do not normally use napkins. They make do with a handkerchief or face flannel. Many just make a token wipe with their hands. Hotels and restaurants catering for foreigners will provide napkins.

nationality guójí [gwor-jee]
 (*for Chinese minorities*) shǎoshù mínzú [show-shoo min-dzoo]

NATIONALITY

It is easy to express nationality in Chinese. The word **rén** [run], person, is simply added to the name of the country. For example:

> **China** Zhōngguo
> **Chinese** Zhōngguo ren
>
> **Japan** Rìben
> **Japanese** Rìben ren
>
> **Britain** Yīngguo
> **British** Yīngguo ren
>
> **France** Fǎguo
> **French** Fǎguo ren
>
> **America** Měiguo
> **American** Měiguo ren

Nationality has a second meaning inside China: 94 per cent of the population are ethnically Chinese **Hàn**, but the remainder are from minority nationalities (**shǎoshù mínzú**), who have their own cultures and languages. They will also learn standard Chinese at school and will have to be fluent in it if they are to get on. Most live in the border regions of the north-west and south-west, but you may well encounter them in Beijing and other major cities. These are some of the most important minorities (the **zú** after their names just means nationality) :

Huízú	Chinese Muslims, found all over China, but especially in Ningxia and in the Beijing area (*see also* MUSLIMS)
Zàngzú	Tibetans
Měngguzú	Mongolians, mostly in the Nei Menggu (Inner Mongolian) Autonomous Region
Wéiwúěrzú	Uighurs, from Xinjiang in the north-west
Cháoxiānzú	Koreans, in the north-east near the border with Korea
Miáozú	From Guangxi province in the south-west

natural (*flavour, taste*) tiānrán(de) [tyen-rahn(der)]

near jìn
   is it near here? lí zhèr jìn ma? [lee jer jin mah]
   is it near Beijing? lí Běijīng jìn ma?
   do you stop near ...? zai ... fùjìn tíngchē ma? [dzI foo-jin ting-cher mah]
   the nearest ... zuìjìn(de) ... [dzway-jin]
   where is the nearest ...? zhèikuàir zuìjìn de ... zai nǎr? [jay-kwIr dzway-jin der ... dzI nar]

necessary bìyào(de) [bee-yow(der)]

neck bózi [boh-dzur]

need: I need ... wǒ xūyào ... [wor syew-yow]
   do you need ...? nǐ xūyào ... ma?

needle zhēng [jung]
   needle and thread zhēng xiàn [jung syen]

NEGATIVES
To change all verbs (but one) which have a present tense reference from positive to negative, you simply put the word **bù** [boo], which means 'not' (and can sometimes mean 'no'), before the verb:

   he is going to Beijing
   tā qù Běijīng
   [tah chyew bay-jing]

   he is not going to Beijing
   tā bú qù Běijīng

   I'll buy this
   wó mǎi zhèige

   I won't buy this
   wǒ bù mǎi zhèige

   he is British
   tā shi Yīngguo ren

   he isn't British
   tā bú shi Yīngguo ren

Bù is normally in the fourth tone (*see* TONES) but before another fourth tone it turns into a second tone. To see why, try to say two fourth tones consecutively!

The exception to the rule that you make the negative with **bù** is the common verb **yǒu** [yoh], which means 'to have' or 'there is/are'. This is always negated by **méi** [may] (and never by **bù**):

   we have a map of Shanghai
   wǒmen yǒu Shànghǎi dìtú
   [wor-mun yoh shahng-hI dee-too]

we haven't any maps of Shanghai
wŏmen méi yŏu Shànghǎi dìtú

there is a telephone in this room
zhèige fángjiān yŏu diànhuà
[jay-ger fahng-jyen yoh dyen-hwah]

there is no telephone in this room
zhèige fángjiān méi yŏu diànhuà

Méi or **méi yŏu** is also used to express the negative of all verbs being used with a past tense reference (*see* PAST TENSE):

he didn't go
tā méi qù
[tah may chyew]

his letter didn't arrive
tāde xìn méi lái
[tah-der syin may lI]

I didn't buy that map
wŏ méi mǎi nèizhāng dìtú
[wor may mI nay-jahng dee-too]

See also IMPERATIVES.

negotiations tánpàn [tahn-pahn]

neither: which one? – neither yào něi yíge? – něi yíge yě bú yào [yow nah yee-ger – nah yee-ger yeh boo yow]
neither do I wó yě bù

Nepal Níbóěr [nee-boh-er]

Nepalese (*adjective*) Níbóěr(de) [nee-boh-er(der)]
(*noun*) Níbóěr ren [nee-boh-er run]

nervous jǐnzhāng [jin-jahng]

net price jìngjià [jing-jyah]

never juébúhuì [jew-eh-boo-hway]

new xīn(de) [syin(der)]

New Year xīnnián [syin-nyen]

NEW YEAR

The Western New Year on 1 January is celebrated with a day's holiday in China, although New Year's Eve is not celebrated. But Chinese New Year, the Spring Festival **chūnjié**, is the most important event of the year both in China and Chinese communities abroad. It is celebrated in late January/early February. Houses are cleaned and swept for the start of the New Year, rather like spring-cleaning in the West.

According to Chinese traditional beliefs, the household Kitchen God (**Zàoshén** or **Zàowángyé**) makes his annual visit to heaven to report on the family at New Year. People usually leave an offering of food over the kitchen range. The Kitchen God eats it and it stops him from making a bad report on the family. This does not figure in the modern socialist ethic, but the tradition of decorating the house to impress him continues. This is usually done with red paper (red being the colour for luck) and quotations in classical couplets written in black on red paper are pasted up. Red envelopes containing money are handed out to children when they **kowtow** to their elders (touching the ground with their forehead).

Chinese New Year is also a time when hundreds of thousands of Chinese travel to be at home with their families, and railway stations are crowded to bursting point, with many extra trains laid on. Most New Year activities are family ones – visiting relatives and neighbours, letting off fireworks and, most important of all, eating. This is a time for buying special delicacies and extra meat. Northerners traditionally make **jiǎozi** [jyow-dzur] to eat at New Year. Whole groups of people get together to make these **jiǎozi** – or spicy meat and vegetable pasties – some rolling the pastry for the skins, others mixing the filling and everyone joining in the activity. Visitors, especially business visitors, should avoid coming to China during the period from a week before to a week after New Year as it is very difficult to arrange anything at this time. *See* CALENDAR.

New Zealand Xīnxīlán [syin-syee-lahn]

news (*on TV etc.*) xīnwén [syin-wun]
 evening news wǎnjiān xīnwén [wahn-jyen syin-wun]
 is there any news? yǒu xiāoxi ma? [yoh syow-syee mah]

NEWS

News and information are carefully monitored and controlled by the state. Although there is far more information available now than there was in the 1960s or 1970s, the government still sees news as having an important part to play in promoting socialism and whatever policies or slogans are currently in favour. Radio and TV news bulletins are in Chinese, of course, but there are two exceptions.

Beijing has a TV news bulletin in English at 10.10 p.m. followed by a film or documentary programme and this is available in hotels for foreigners. The radio service for the capital Beijing has English broadcasts from 7 o'clock in the evening on 1251 kHz on medium wave and 91.55 MHz on FM. It is also available on 1296 and 1584 kHz in Shanghai and Guangzhou respectively.

newspaper bào(zhǐ) [bow(jur)]　报纸
    English newspapers Yīngwén bào(zhǐ) [ying-wun bow(jur)]

NEWSPAPERS

All newspapers and magazines in China have to register with the government and their contents are strictly controlled, although some journalists in the 1980s have succeeded in developing a campaigning style and exposing corruption and maladministration. With one exception, all newspapers are printed in Chinese. The most important are **Rénmín Rìbào**, *People's Daily*, which is the organ of the Communist Party's Central Committee and gives authoritative statements of the Party's policy, and **Guāngmíng Rìbào**, *Guangming Daily*, which is widely read by scientists and the intelligentsia in general. Party and government officials have for years got their information about developments outside China from a paper called **Cānkǎo Xiāoxi** (*Reference News*). This has limited circulation but has recently been made more widely available. Every province and city has its local paper and there are both daily and evening papers and specialist sheets for sports, TV etc.

The one newpaper in English is the *China Daily*, first issued in 1981 and published in London, New York and Hong Kong as well as in Beijing. It employs some Western journalists although it has by no means adopted Western standards of reporting or judgements about what makes news. *China Daily* does, however, sometimes contain information and views not found in the Chinese-language press.

next xià yíge [syah yee-ger]
    at the next bus stop xià yízhàn [syah yee-jahn]
    next year míng nián [ming nyen]
    next time xià yícì [syah yee-tsur]
    next to the hotel fàndiàn gébì [fahn-dyen ger-bee]

nice (*person, meal, day*) hǎo [how]
  that's very nice of you nǐ zhēng hǎo [nee jung how]

night wǎnshang [wahn-shahng]
  good night (*going to bed*) wǎn'ān [wahn-ahn]

no bù [boo]
  there's no toilet paper wèishēngzhǐ méi yǒu le [way-shung-jee may yoh ler]
  I have no ... wǒ méi yǒu ... [wor may yoh]

NO

There is no one word equivalent to 'no' (or indeed to 'yes') in Chinese. **Bù** on its own is used sometimes and will be clear enough in an emergency.

    The normal way of saying 'no' in answer to a question is to repeat the verb in the question but with the word **bù** in front of it:

  are you coming?
  nǐ lái ma?
  [nee lI mah]

  no
  bù lái

  do you like Chinese tea?
  ní xǐhuān Zhōngguo chá ma?
  [nee syee-hwahn joong-gwor chah mah]

  no
  bù xǐhuān

  is he Chinese?
  tā shi Zhōngguo ren ma?
  [tah shur joong-gwor run mah]

  no
  bú shì

  do you want to buy this?
  zhèige ní mǎibumǎi?
  [jay-ger nee mI-boo-mI]

  no
  bù mǎi

nobody méi(yǒu)rén [may(yoh)run]

none shénme yě méiyǒu [shun-mah yer may-yoh]

normal zhèngcháng(de) [jung-chahng(der)]

north běi [bay]
  in the north běifāng [bay-fahng]

nose bízi [bee-dzur]

not bù [boo]

>**not for me, thanks** wǒ bú yào, xièxie [wor boo yow syeh-syeh]
>
>**not Tuesday** bú shi xīngqī'èr [boo shur sying-chee-er]
>
>(*Tuesday won't do*) xīngqī'èr bù xíng [sying-chee-er boo sying]
>
>**he's not here** tā búzài zhèr [tah boo-dzI jer]
>
>**I'm not Mr Brown, I'm ...** wǒ bú shi Bùláng xiānsheng, wǒ jiào ... [wor boo shur boo-lahng syen-shung, wor jyow]
>
>*See* NEGATIVES.

notebook bǐjìběnr [bee-jee-bunr]

NOTEBOOKS

At meetings, it is very common for people to take copious notes, far more than you would expect in the West. Notebooks are often backed in bright plastic and you should look out for them in the shops as authentic souvenirs.

nothing méi yǒu shénme [may yoh shun-mah]

NOUNS

Chinese nouns do not change or take any endings to form the singular or plural. Context usually makes this clear (*but see* PLURALS). There are no genders.

November shíyīyue [shur-yee-yew-eh]

now xiànzài [syen-dzI]

number hàomǎ [how-mah]

>**what number is it?** duōshao hào? [dwor-show how]

NUMBERS

Here are the Chinese numbers from 1 to 20:

一	1	yī	[yee]
二	2	èr	[er]
	or	**liǎng**	[lyahng] (see below)
三	3	sān	[sahn]
四	4	sì	[sur]
五	5	wǔ	[woo]
六	6	liù	[lyoh]
七	7	qī	[chee]
八	8	bā	[bah]
九	9	jiǔ	[jyoh]
十	10	shí	[shur]

If you learn the basic numbers 1 to 10, you know enough to make all the numbers up to 99. For the teens you say 10 and follow it with the unit:

十一	11	shíyī
十二	12	shíèr
十三	13	shísān
十四	14	shísì
十五	15	shíwŭ
十六	16	shíliù
十七	17	shíqī
十八	18	shíbā
十九	19	shíjiŭ
二十	20	èrshí

For multiples of 10, it is the other way round – you say 10 preceded by the number (for example 20 is 2 – 10):

二十	20	èrshí
三十	30	sānshí
四十	40	sìshí

and so on.

For multiples of 10 plus units, just add the units:

五十一	51	wŭshíyī
六十二	62	liùshíèr
	etc.	
百	100	băi	[bI]

For multiples of 100 the same rules apply:

二百	200	èrbăi
三百	300	sānbăi
三百五十七	357	sānbăi wŭshíqī
	etc.	

千	1,000	qiān	[chyen]
万	10,000	wàn	[wahn]
亿	100,000,000	yì	[yee]

(10,000 × 10,000 or **yíwànwàn**, useful when talking about the population of China).

Large numbers are counted either in units of ten thousand **wàn** or in units of a hundred million **yì**. (Confusion often arises in oral translation as the interpreter switches between the two systems of counting.)

If you are counting things or people, there must be a classifier between the number and the noun (*see* CLASSIFIERS):

three English people
sān ge Yīngguo ren

seven books
qī běn shū

One peculiarity is that you cannot use **èr** in this way when talking about two things or two people. A special word, **liǎng** [lyahng], is used instead:

two people
liǎng ge rén

two books
liáng běn shū

Ordinal numbers

Ordinal numbers are formed by putting **dì** in front of the cardinal numbers:

one	**yī**
first	**dìyī** [dee-yee]
two	**èr**
second	**dì'èr** [dee-er]
three	**sān**
third	**dìsān** [dee-sahn]
etc.	

O

October shíyue [shur-yew-eh]

of de [der]

OF

The very common Chinese particle **de** also works in many cases as a translation for 'of'. Chinese, however, makes an inversion to the English word order:

the manager of the hotel
fàndiàn de jīnglǐ
(*literally: hotel of manager*)

the population of China
Zhōngguo de rénkǒu
(*literally: China of population*)

off (*machine*) guān shang le [gwahn shahng ler]
(*food*) huàile [hwI-ler]
I'm off wó zǒule [wor dzoh-ler]

offer (*noun*) bàojià [bow-jyah]
we can offer ... wǒmen kéyi tígōng ... [wor-mun ker-yee tee-goong]

office (*workplace*) bàngōngshì [bahn-goong-shur]

official (*noun*) xíngzhèng guānyuán [sying-juhng gwahn-yew-ahn]

often jīngcháng [jing-chahng]

oil yóu [yoh]
(*on food*) shíyòng yóu [shur-yoong yoh]

OK āokài [ow-kI], hǎo [how]

old (*person*) lǎo [low]
(*thing*) juì [jway]
how old are you? nín duōdà niánling? [neen doh-dah nyen-ling]
(*to children*) ni jǐsuì le? [nee jee-sway ler]
(*to old people*) nín duōdà niánjì le? [neen doh-dah nyen-jee ler]
See CALENDAR.

old-fashioned (*thing*) guòshí(der) [gwor-shur-der]
(*person*) shǒujiù(de) [shoh-jyoh-der]

on (zai) ... shang [(dzI) ... shahng]
on Tuesday xīngqi'èr [sying-chee-er]

is it on? (*machine etc.*) kāi le? [kI-ler]
a book on China guānyú Zhōngguó de shū [gwahn-yew joong-gwor der shoo]

Like all prepositions in Chinese, **shang** is really a postposition, and comes after the noun it refers to:

> **on the table**
> zai zhuōzi shang

To say 'on a bicycle', Chinese uses **qí**:

> **he is coming on his bike**
> tā qí zìxíngchē lái
> [ta chee dzur-sying-cher lI]

one: one person yíge ren [yee-ger run]
the first one dì yīge

ONE

To say 'one ...', you use **yi** followed by the appropriate classifier and then the noun (*see* CLASSIFIERS):

> **one book**
> yì běn shū
> [yee bun shoo]

> **one glass of beer**
> yì bēi píjiŭ
> [yee bay pee-jyoh]

The normal tone for **yi** is the fourth tone as in **yì**. But if another fourth tone follows it, **yì** becomes **yí** (second tone) (*see* TONES):

> **one yuan**
> yí kuài qián
> [yee kwI chyen]

only zhíyŏu [jur-yoh]

open (*adjective*) kāi(de) [kI(der)]
are they open tomorrow? (tāmen) míngtian kāiménr ma? [tah-mun ming-tyen kI-munr ma]
when do you open? nĭmen shénme shíhou kāiménr?
[nee-mun shun-mah shur-hoh kI-munr]
can I open the window? wŏ kéyi dăkāi chuāng ma?
[wor ker-yee dah-kI chwahng ma]

opera gējù [ger-jew]
Peking Opera jīngjù [jing-jew]

operation (*in hospital*) shŏushù [shoh-shoo]

operator (*telephone*) zŏngjī [dzoong-jee]

opinion yìjiàn [yee-jyen]
in my opinion yī wŏ kàn [yee wor kahn]

opposite (*position*) duìmiànr [dway-myenr]
  (*opinion*) (zhèng) xiāngfǎn [(jung) syahng-fahn]

or huòzhě [hwor-zher]

orange juice júzi zhī [jew-dzur jur]

order (*in business*) dìnghuò
  thank you for your order xièxie nínde dìnghuò
  [syeh-syeh neen-der ding-hwor]

order number (*for each customer*) gùkè hàomǎ [goo-ker
  how-mah]
  (*for each order*) dìngdān hàomǎ

organize: well organized zǔzhīde hén hǎo [dzoo-jur-der
  hun how]
  poorly organized zǔzhīde bù hǎo

other qítā [chee-tah]
  the other one lìng yíge [ling yee-ger]

our, ours wǒmende [wor-mun-der]
  wǒmende can mean either 'our' or 'ours':

      our room
      wǒmende fángjiān
      [wor-mun-der fahng-jyen]
      this is ours
      zhèi shi wǒmende
      [jay shur wor-mun-der]

out (*lights*) guān shang le [gwahn shahng ler]
  she's out (*of house etc.*) tā chūqu le [tah choo-chyew
  ler]
  it will be out next month (*new model etc.*) xiàge yuè
  zhèi jiù huì jiànshì [syah-ger yew-eh jay jyoh hway
  jyen-shur]

over (*finished*) wánle [wahn-ler]
  over forty sìshi duō [sur-shur dwor]
  over there zai nàr [dzI nar]

overcoat dàyī [dah-yee]

overnight (*travel*) guòyè [gwor-yeh]

oversleep: I'm afraid I overslept wó kǒngpà shuìguòtóu
  le [wor koong-pah shway-gwor-toh ler]

owe: we owe you . . . wǒmen qiàn nǐmen . . . [wor-mun
  chyen nee-mun]
  you owe us . . . nǐmen qiàn wǒmen . . .

own: my own . . . wǒ zìjǐde . . . [wor dzur-jee-der]
  your own . . . nǐ zìjǐde . . .

owner suóyóuzhě [swor-yoh-jer]

P

packet bāo [bow]
   a packet of . . . yìbāo . . . [yee-bow]

paddy field dàotián [dow-tyen]

pagoda tǎ [tah]

pain téng [tung]

panda xióngmāo [syoong-mow]

paper zhǐ [jur]
   (*newspaper*) bàozhǐ [bow-jur]
   a piece of paper yìzhāng zhǐ [yee-jahng jur]

pardon? qǐng zài shuō yíbiàn [ching dzI shwor yee-byen]
   (*literally: please say that again*)

parents fùmǔ [foo-moo]

park (*noun*) gōngyuán [goong-yew-ahn]

part (*noun*) bùfen [boo-fun]

PARTICLES
Particles are words which have no inherent meaning by themselves but which are used to modify the sense of the sentence in which they occur. The commonest particles are the following:

MA
This is used to turn a statement into a question:

   tā lái
   he is coming

   tā lái ma?
   is he coming

BA
This has two basic uses. It is often the equivalent of 'shall we' or 'let's' in English, being used to make suggestions:

   wǒmen zǒu ba
   shall we go?, let's go

It can also be used in the type of question which automatically assumes that the answer will be 'yes':

   tā shi Zhōngguo ren ba?
   he's Chinese, isn't he?

BĂ

This particle, not to be confused with **ba** above (no tone), is used to mark a word which is the object of a sentence when it is brought forward to the beginning of the sentence in order to be given more emphasis:

> **wó bă hùzhào diūle**
> I've lost my passport
> (*literally: I (bă) passport lose (le)*)

LE

This is a very widely used particle. It has two main functions. One is to indicate that an action has been completed. In this case it is a verb particle and is written in Pinyin joined up with the verb:

> **tā láile**
> he came, he has come

This action need not necessarily be in the past. For example, given the appropriate context:

> **tā láile**

can also mean:

> here he comes!

Le can also be used to show that a change of circumstances has taken place:

> **xià yŭ le**
> it's raining

The implication in this last sentence is that it is raining now and that it wasn't before. The sentence:

> **xià yŭ**

can just mean 'it rains' as in making general statements about the weather. This is, in fact, another aspect of the particle **le** – it can be seen as being in a way related to the distinction made in philosophy between the general and particular, with the addition of the particle **le** indicating that a particular occurrence is being referred to as opposed to a general statement. Some examples will make this clear:

General statement:

> **wŏ yūnchuán**
> I get seasick

Particular statement using particle **le**:

> **wŏ yūnchuánle**
> I feel seasick

General statement:

tā jìdù
he's jealous (is a jealous person)

Particular statement:

tā jìdùle
he's jealous (at the moment)

Note also the difference made by the use of **le** in the following two contrasted sentences:

I've been in China for two months
wǒ zai Zhōngguo dāile liǎngge yùele

I was in China for two months
wǒ zai Zhōngguo dāile liǎngge yùe

A

This particle is a common sentence or phrase ending. Sometimes it adds emphasis and sometimes it just rounds off a sentence:

lái a!
do drop in (when you have time)!

shéi a?
who is it?

NE

This has two main functions. It can indicate that an action is continuing:

tā zai déng wǒmen ne
he is waiting for us (so let's hurry)

It can also have the meaning of 'how about?':

wǒ bú tài máng – nǐ ne?
I'm not very busy – how about you?

GUO [gwor]

This particle is added after verbs when you want to make it clear whether you have or have not had a particular experience. It can be seen as similar to the perfect tense in English:

nǐ qù guo Zhōngguo ma?
have you (ever) been to China?

qù guo
yes

méi qù guo
no

DE

One particle pronounced **de** is used to form constructions equivalent to adverb constructions in English – *see* ADVERBS.

Another particle also pronounced **de** but written with a different Chinese character is so common that it appears in almost every sentence. One of its functions is to indicate possession and its simplest usage can be seen in the transformation of the personal pronouns:

wǒ I
nǐ you
tā he, she

into the possessive adjectives:

wǒde my
nǐde your
tāde his, hers

The same particle also does the job which the English relative pronouns 'who', 'which', 'that' do in linking parts of a sentence:

zhìzào nèiliang qìchē de gōngsī
the company which manufactures that car
(*literally: manufacture that car (de) company*)

mái wǒmen chánpǐn de nèi wèi xiānsheng
the gentleman who is buying our products
(*literally: buy our products (de) that gentleman*)

Note the change in the word order when this particle is used. This particle **de** also has a very general application in this usage. It can mean not only 'who', 'which' etc. but is used to link 'when' and 'where' to the rest of the sentence:

wǒmen dào zhè lái de shíhou
when we got here

nǐ cóng nár mäi de?
where did you buy it?

partner (*in business*) **màoyì huǒbàn** [mow-yee hwor-bahn]

party (*political*) **dǎng** [dahng]
let's have a party wǒmen yíkuàir jùju, zěnmeyàng?
[wor-mun yee-kwIr jyew-jyew dzun-mah-yahng]

PASSIVE

Passives are normally avoided in spoken Standard Chinese, but there are ways of making them if you must:

1. By using **bèi** [bay] which does not have a meaning of its own, but just marks the passive:

the police arrested him
jǐngchá dàibǔ le tā

he was arrested
tā bèi dàibǔ le

he cheated me
tā piàn le wǒ

I was cheated
wǒ bèi piàn le

This way of forming the passive tends to be used when something unpleasant or unwanted happens. Instead of **bèi**, you can also use **jiào** [jyow], **ràng** [rahng] and **gěi** [gay] with exactly the same meaning.

2. By using **shì ... de** [shur ... der] to emphasize the agent in an action:

this report was written by my colleague
zhèige bàogào shi wǒ tóngshì xiě de

this hotel was recommended by Mr Zheng
zhèige fàndiàn shi Zhāng xiānsheng jièshào de

passport hùzhào [hoo-jow] 护照

past: past the crossroads/hotel guòle shízì lùkǒur/ fàndiàn [gwor-ler shur-dzur loo-kohr/fahn-dyen]

PAST TENSE
Chinese verbs have no true markers of tense. Chinese grammar tends to stress whether an action has been either:

    (i) completed
    (ii) not completed

rather than whether it took place at a particular time in the past, present or future (*see also* VERBS).

    If it is necessary to be precise about the time of an action, you can add a time word (such as 'yesterday', 'last month' etc.) to the sentence:

he came to Beijing yesterday
tā zuótian láide Běijīng

If an action in the past was completed, or you are noting that it was not, then the markers of completion **le** and non-completion **méi(yǒu)** can be used:

I lived there for two years
wǒ zài nàr zhù le liǎngnián

I did not go to the factory
wǒ méi qù gōngchǎng

Beware of thinking that these are easy ways of forming a past tense. **Le** can also be used to describe an action that will be completed in the future (*see* PARTICLES).

    The fact that a language has no past tense might seem puzzling at first to a Westerner who is used to the idea of tenses. But, on closer analysis, the absence of a past tense as such is perhaps not such a lack after all. For example:

I don't know
wǒ bù zhīdào

I didn't know
wǒ bù zhīdào

What you are doing in making these two utterances is one and the same thing – you are expressing a lack of knowledge. How important is the time aspect? Pidgin English would say 'I not know' for both and be perfectly comprehensible. As we have seen, if it should be important to place an action at a particular point in the past, then Chinese uses a time word such as 'yesterday', 'last year' and indicates past tense in this way. If the time aspect is logically of no significance, then Chinese does not feel obliged to express what is redundant. Here are some more examples:

I can't hear
wǒ tīng bú jiàn

I couldn't hear
wǒ tīng bú jiàn

it doesn't work
zhè bù gōngzuò

it didn't work
zhè bù gōngzuò

In each of these contrasted pairs the important aspect of the statement is either the fact of not being able to hear or of something not working. If you need to put that in the past, then add a word such as 'yesterday' etc.

path xiǎolù [syow-loo]

pavement rénxíng dào [run-sying dow]

pay fù(qián) [foo-(chyen)]
  can I pay now, please? wǒ xiànzài fùqián, xíng ma? [wor syen-dzI foo-chyen sying mah]
  I'll pay for this zhèige yóu wǒ lái fù [jay-ger wor II foo]

payment zhīfù [jur-foo]

pen gāngbǐ [gahng-bee]

pencil qiānbǐ [chyen-bee]

people rénmín [run-min]
  a lot of people xǔduō rén [syew-dwor-run]

People's Republic of China Zhōnghuá Rénmín Gònghéguó [joong-hwah run-min goong-her-gwor]

pepper (*spice*) hújiáo [hoo-jow]

per: per night méi wǎnshang [may wahn-shahng]
 per day měi tiān [may-yee tyen]

per cent bǎifēn bǐ [bI-fun bee]
 25 per cent bǎifēn zhī èrshíwǔ [bI-fun jur er-shur-woo]
 a 10 per cent discount bǎifēn zhī shí de zhékòu [bI-fun jur shur der jur-koh]

perfect (*adjective*) juéduì bàng [jyew-eh-dway bahng]

PERFECT TENSE *see* PAST TENSE

perfume xiāngshuǐr [syahng-shway'r]

perhaps kěnéng [ker-nung]

permit (*noun: entry permit etc.*) xúkě zhèng [syew-ker jung]
 travel permit lǚxíng zhèng [lyew-sying jung]

person rén [run]

PERSONAL PRONOUNS

The basic personal pronouns in Chinese are:

singular		*plural*	
I	wǒ [wor]	**we**	wǒmen [wor-mun]
you	nǐ [nee]	**you**	nǐmen [nee-mun]
he/she	tā [tah]	**they**	tāmen [tah-mun]

There is also a polite form for 'you' which is **nín** [neen] in the singular and **nínmen** [neen-mun] in the plural.

Note that **tā** can mean either he or she (and sometimes it). Although this word is pronounced in exactly the same way, it is written with different characters for each sense.

Personal pronouns in Chinese do not undergo any changes for different cases. So, for example, Chinese uses the same word – **wǒ** – for 'I' and 'me' and the same word – **wǒmen** – for 'we' and 'us' etc. Here are some examples of this:

 I saw him
 wǒ kàndao tā le

 he saw me
 tā kàndao wǒ le

we met her
wŏmen jiàndao tā le

she met us
tā jiàndao wŏmen le

petrol qìyóu [chee-yoh]

petrol station jiāyóu zhàn [jyah-yoh jahn]

PETROL STATIONS

Once a rarity, petrol stations are now springing up all over China to accommodate the millions of cars, lorries, minibuses, motorcycles and tractors that are taking to the roads. Unless you become one of the privileged few Westerners allowed to drive in China you will probably never go inside a petrol station. Safety regulations insist that all passengers wait outside while the driver takes the car in to fill up.

photograph zhàopiān [jow-pyen]

PHOTOGRAPHS

Photography is now a major hobby in China and there are several specialist photographic magazines and regular exhibitions at art galleries. At beauty spots and tourist sites, Chinese-made cameras can be seen alongside foreign imports. Chinese tend to photograph each other against a famous landmark rather than the landmark itself, and your host or guide will probably be happy to do the same for you. There are professional photographers who will photograph you with a camel at the Great Wall or your child next to a plastic panda in Beijing zoo. Chinese and imported film is available and can be left for developing and printing with no difficulty in the main tourist hotels.

The do's and don't's are usually fairly obvious. Like all Communist countries, and most which are not, China is highly sensitive about any places or objects connected with defence. These should not be photographed. The definition of defence is wider than in the West and includes bridges and civil aircraft and airports. It is sometimes difficult to know where to draw the line – apparently it is quite acceptable to photograph a Yangzi ferry in mid-river, but not when it approaches its moorings. Photography from the air is not allowed either. Old people, particularly in the countryside, may also be unhappy about being photographed either for superstitious reasons or just because they feel it is an invasion of privacy. Tourists have often given Polaroid photos to Chinese they met. This has become something of a cliché and it is often irrelevant now that so many Chinese take photographs themselves, but it is still popular with children.

picture (*painting, drawing*) huà [hwah]

piece kuàir, piànr [kwIr, pyen'r]
   a piece of . . . *see* CLASSIFIERS.

pig zhū [joo]

pillow zhèntou [jun-toh]

pin dàtóuzhēn [dah-toh-jun]

PINYIN

Pīnyīn, the system of spelling Chinese sounds used in this book, is short for **Hànyǔ Pīnyīn**, which just means phonetic Chinese. It was developed in the 1950s on the basis of a Latinized script tested before the Second World War and is now used as a learning tool in textbooks for foreigners and for speakers of regional forms of Chinese who are learning Standard Chinese.

Most Chinese are not familiar with Pinyin. The exceptions are teachers, particularly in primary schools, and young children and teenagers who are learning it, partly to help them with their study of English.

You will not see much Pinyin written in China. Everything is in Chinese characters. But there is a Pinyin transcription on street signs in large cities which is very useful for finding your way around. And the name of a newspaper is usually in Pinyin as well as characters. Also the names of some shops. Since the 1950s, there has been a running debate about whether Pinyin should replace characters for writing Chinese, but there is no sign of this happening in the foreseeable future (*see also* ALPHABET, CHARACTERS).

Since Pinyin uses English letters in a special way, the following conversion table may be of use:

c	ts
q	ch
x	sh
zh	j (as in 'Janet')
ai	as in 'Thai'
ao	as in in 'now' or 'Mao'

e	as in 'her'
ei	as in 'weight'
en	as in 'open'
eng	with the 'e' as in 'her'
i	either as in 'Maria'
	or if coming after c, ch, r, s, sh, z, zh
	then like the 'i' sound in 'sir'
ia	like the 'ya' in 'yard'
ie	like the 'ye' in 'yellow'
iu	like the 'yo' in 'yo-yo'
o	as in 'for'
ou	as in 'Joe' or 'dough'
ong	with the 'o' as in 'who'
u	either as in 'soon'
	or if coming after j, q, x then like the 'u' sound in French 'du' or German 'über'
ü	as in French 'du' or German 'über'
ua, uai	with the 'u' like 'w'
ui	as in 'way'
uo	as in 'war'

pipe (*to smoke*) yāndǒu [yen-doh]
    (*for liquid*) shuíguǎnr [shway-gwahn-r]

place (*noun*) dìfang [dee-fahng]

PLACE NAMES
If you examine them carefully, you will see that
Chinese place names often contain historical and
geographical information. They are frequently combinations of the points of the compass:

> **east**
> dōng
> [doong]

> **west**
> xī
> [syee]

> **south**
> nán
> [nahn]

> **north**
> běi
> [bay]

(that is the normal Chinese order) with other
geographical features.

Shāndōng [shahn-doong] (the name of a province to
the east of Běijīng) means 'to the east of the

mountains' and **Shānxī** [shahn-syee], 'to the west of the mountains'. Two of the large central Chinese provinces are called **Húnán** [hoo-nahn] and **Húběi** [hoo-bay], which mean respectively 'north and south of the lakes'.

Jīng is the word for a capital city and **Běijīng** and **Nánjīng** were the northern and southern capitals of the Ming dynasty.

plastic sùliào [soo-lyow]

plate pánzi [pahn-dzur]

platform zhàntái [jahn-tI]　站台
   which platform? jǐhào zhàntái? [jee-how jahn-tI]
   is this the platform for ...? dào ... qù, shì zhèige zhàntái ma? [dow ... chyew shur jay-ger jahn-tI mah]

pleasant língrén yúkuài [ling-run yew-kwI]

please: can you please ...? máfan nín néng ... ma? [mah-fahn neen nung ... mah]
   would you like a cup of tea? – yes, please hē bēi chá ba? – hǎo, xièxie [her bay chah bah – how syeh-syeh]
   please do qǐng [ching]

PLEASE

If you are inviting or politely requesting someone to do something, **qǐng** is a useful word:

> **please have some tea**
> qǐng hē chá
> [ching her chah]

> **please go first**
> nín xiān qǐng
> [neen syen ching]

You can also use **máfan**, which is roughly equivalent to 'may I trouble you?', where in English we would use 'please':

> **please may I have some tea?**
> máfan nǐ lái yìbēi chá
> [mah-fahn nee lI yee-bay chah]

To ask someone not to do something, **qǐng** is also used with **bié** [byeh], **bù** [boo] or **búyào** [boo-yow] meaning 'don't':

> **please don't be so polite**
> qǐng ni bié kèqi
> [ching nee byeh ker-chee]

> **please don't be anxious**
> qǐng ni bié zhāojí

[ching nee byeh jow-jee]
plenty xǔduō [syew-dwor]
　plenty of ... xǔduō ...

PLURALS

Chinese nouns, like all other Chinese words, are invariable; they cannot take any endings. So for example:

　　shū

means

　'a book' or 'books'

depending on the context.

　　wǒ qù shūdiàn mǎi shū qù

can mean

　I am going to the bookshop to buy books/a book.

If you feel it is necessary to be more specific you can put in **yìxiē shū** for 'some books' or **yìběn shū** for 'one book'.

The plural marker **men** [mun] (which is used for personal pronouns) can be added to a few nouns which refer to people, so you will come across:

　　xiānsheng/xiānshengmen gentleman/gentlemen
　　nǚshi/nǚshimen lady/ladies
　　xuésheng/xuéshengmen student/students
　　péngyou/péngyoumen friend/friends

pocket kǒudàir [koh-dIr]

point: please point to it qǐng zhí gei wǒ kàn [ching jur gay wor kahn]
　two point five èr diánr wǔ [er dyen-r woo]
　that's a good point zhèige jiànyì hénhǎo [jay-ger jyen-yee hun-how]

POINTING

Pointing to what you want in a shop or a restaurant is considered a polite and efficient way of getting things and is only a problem for Chinese travelling overseas when they have to learn not to do it.

police jǐngchá [jing-chah]

POLICE

The police are employed by the Bureau of Public Security, the **Gōngānjú**. The ones you will generally see around are the traffic police directing the traffic from raised stands at crossroads. Or they may be driving around in blue and white cars, jeeps or motorcycle and sidecar combinations with the word **Gongan** written in Pinyin. There are many other branches, mostly plain clothes. Foreign visitors are unlikely to need the police but the hotel or China Travel will have a liaison officer if it is necessary. The police service is not a suitable topic for conversation; it is looked on as part of the defence of the state.

policeman jǐngchá [jing-chah]

polite kèqi [ker-chee]

politics zhèngzhi [jung-jur]

POLITICS

On one level, politics are unavoidable in China. You will be made aware of the current political campaigns or slogans such as:

> **sìge xiàndàihuà**
> [sur-ger syen-dI-hwah]
> four modernizations (agriculture, industry, defence, science and technology)

> **fǎnduì zīchǎnjiējí zìyóuhuà**
> [fahn-dway dzur-chahn-jyeh-jee dzur-yoh-hwah]
> oppose bourgeois liberalism

Such slogans are all round you in newspapers, on hoardings and on the radio and TV news and the Chinese have learned to interpret them and adjust their way of life accordingly. Since 1949, politics has affected people's private lives in a way Westerners find difficult to comprehend. Chinese grow up learning to cope with these shifts in political direction.

On another level, the type of political discussion common in the West is difficult in China, particularly if it throws doubt on the Chinese socialist system. Students and others who are genuinely interested in comparing China with the West may initiate discussions, but don't force them on your guide or host.

population rénkǒu [run-koh]
   the population of China Zhōngguo de rénkǒu [joong-gwor der run-koh]

pork zhūròu [joo-roh]

PORK

Pork is possibly the most popular meat in China and the most likely filling for your **bāozi** [bow-dzur] or stuffed steamed bread roll. Even in the days of the communes, farming families were able to keep a pig of their own. Chinese Muslims – and there are far more than generally realized – avoid pork of course.

port (*for ships*) gángkǒu [gahng-koh]

porter (*in hotel: for bags*) xíngli yuán [sying-lee yew-ahn]

POSSESSIVE ADJECTIVES

These are formed by adding the possessive particle **de** to the personal pronouns:

I	wǒ	[wor]	**my**	wǒde
you	nǐ	[nee]	**your**	nǐde
he/she	tā	[tah]	**his/hers**	tāde
we	wǒmen	[wor-mun]	**our**	wǒmende
you (*pl*)	nǐmen	[nee-mun]	**your** (*pl*)	nǐmende
they	tāmen	[tah-mun]	**their**	tāmende

For example:

> **my passport**
> wǒde yàoshi
> [wor-der yow-shur]

> **your products**
> nǐmende chánpǐn
> [nee-mun-der chahn-pin]

> **their bicycles**
> tāmende zìxíngchē
> [tah-mun-der dzur-sying-cher]

Possessive adjectives can be omitted in Chinese if no ambiguity arises from this. For example:

> **I left my key in my room**
> wó bǎ yàoshi là zai wōli le
> [wor bah yow-shur lah dzI wor-lee ler]
> (*literally: I left key in room*)

When used with words referring to members of a family or things in which there is a degree of personal relationship the **de** can be omitted so that, effectively, the personal pronoun functions as possessive adjective:

> **wó jiějie**
> my (elder) sister

> **tā fùqin**
> his/her father

nǐ dìdi
your (younger) brother

possible kěnéng [ker-nung]
   is it possible to ...? yóu kěnéng ... ma? [yoh ker-nung mah]

post (*verb*) jì [jee]

post office yóujú [yoh-jew]   邮局
Most hotels catering for Westerners will have post office desks.

postcard míngxìnpiàn [ming-sying-pyen]

potatoes tǔdòu [too-doh]

pound (*weight*) bàng [bahng]
   (*sterling*) Yīngbàng [ying-bahng]

prefer: which do you prefer? nǐ gèng xǐhuān nǎge?
[nee gung syee-hwahn nah-ger]
   I prefer ... wǒ gèng xǐhuān ... [wor gung syee-hwahn]

present (*gift*) lǐwù [lee-woo]

PRESENT TENSE

To talk about an action or state that is taking place at the present time you just use the verb on its own. In Chinese there are no endings to be added, so the verb always stays in the same form. Look at the following examples for the verb **gōngzuò** [goong-dzwor], 'to work':

where do you work?
nǐ zai nǎr gōngzuò?
[nee dzI nahr goong-dzwor]

I work in London
wǒ zai Lúndūn gōngzuò
[wor dzI loon-doon goong-dzwor]

he works with us
tā gēn wǒmen yìqǐ gōngzuò
[tah gun wor-mun yee-chee goong-dzwor]

they're working very hard
tāmen gōngzuò de hén nǔlì
[tah-mun goong-dzwor der hun nyew-lee]

If you want to emphasize that an action is going on at this moment, other markers can be added, such as **zài**:

I'm waiting for someone
wǒ zai děng rén
[wor dzI dung run]

president (*of state*) zóngtŏng [dzoong-toong]

pretty piàoliang [pyow-lyahng]

price jiàgé [jyah-ger]
  that's our best price zhèi shi wŏmen néngchū de zuìhăo jiàgé [jay shur wor-mun nung-choo der dzway-how jyah-ger]

private sīrén(de) [sur-run(der)]
  in private (*talk etc.*) sīxià li [sur-syah lee]

probably dàgài [dah-gI]

problem wèntí [wun-tee]
  we've had some problems wŏmen yùdàole xiē wèntí [wor-mun yew-dow-ler syeh wun-tee]
  that's no problem! méi wèntí! [may wun-tee]

product chánpĭn [chahn-pin]

production manager chángzhăng [chahng-jahng]
  (*literally: factory manager*)

professor jiàoshòu [jyow-shoh]

profit lìrùn [lee-roon]

pronounce fāyīn [fah-yin]
  how is it pronounced? zĕnme niàn? [zun-mah nyen]
  See TONES.

PRONOUNS *see* PERSONAL PRONOUNS.

PUBLIC HOLIDAYS

Most Chinese work long hours, with only one day off each week, so public holidays are celebrated enthusiastically. They are also the only times of the year that widely scattered families can get together. The main holidays are:

New Year – 1 January (one day)

Chinese New Year (Spring Festival), which falls in late January/early February according to the Chinese lunar calendar (three days)

May Day (International Labour Day) – 1 May (one day)

National Day, 1 October, anniversary of the day in 1949 when Mao Zedong announced the foundation of the People's Republic of China from the rostrum of Tiananmen, the Gate of Heavenly Peace (two days)

Offices, most factories and some shops are closed during these festivals although food shops do a roaring trade. Coloured lights decorate the main buildings and there are sometimes firework displays and a variety of leisure activities as well as public meetings. *See also* FESTIVALS.

publicity xuānchuán [syew-ahn-chwahn]

pull lā [lah]　拉

pure (*substance*) chún [choon]

push tuī [tway]　推

Q

quality zhìliàng [jur-lyahng]

quality goods (*good quality*) yōuzhì chánpǐn [yoh-jur chahn-pin]

quality control zhìliàng jiǎnchá [jur-lyahng jyen-chah]

quarter sì fēn zhī yī [sur fun jur yee]
(*of year*) jìdu [jee-doo]
See TIME TELLING.

QUESTIONS

There are three common ways of forming questions in Chinese:

(1) Using the particle **ma** [mah]:

> **he is going**
> tā qù
>
> **is he going?**
> tā qù ma?
>
> **he is Chinese**
> tā shi Zhōngguo ren
>
> **is he Chinese?**
> tā shi Zhōngguo ren ma?

(2) Offering a choice between the possible yes or no answers by using the verb on its own and then the verb preceded by **bù** [boo] meaning 'not' (or **méi** [may] if it is the verb **yǒu**). This might sound complicated at first, but in a way it can be seen as similar to the very common English construction in such phrases as 'you are coming, aren't you?' or 'he does live here, doesn't he?' Here are some examples of this way of asking questions in Chinese:

> **tā qù bú qù?**
> is he going?
> (*literally: he go not go?*)
>
> **tā shi bú shi Zhōngguó ren?**
> is he Chinese?
> (*literally: he is not is Chinese person?*)
>
> **nǐ yǒu méi yǒu dìtú?**
> have you got a map?
> (*literally: you have not have map?*)

(3) By using a question word. The most important question words are:

who?	shéi?	[shay]
what?	shénme?	[shun-mah]
where?	nǎr?	[nah]
why?	wèishénme?	[way-shun-mah]
how?	zěnme?	[zun-mah]
when?	shénme shíhou	[shun-mah shur-hoh]

If you are using one of these questions words, you do not add **ma** at the end of a sentence and you do not give a choice of positive and negative verbs. Here are some examples of sentences using these question words (note the word order):

who is she/he?
tā shi shéi?

who's coming?
shéi lái?

what is that?
nà shi shénme?

where is your hotel?
nǐde fàndiàn zai nǎr?

why isn't he coming?
tā wèishénme bù lái?

how are you going?
ní zěnme zǒu?

when will the delegation get to Beijing?
dàibiǎotuán shénme shíhou dào Běijīng?

See also PARTICLES.

quick kuài [kwI]

quickly hěn kuài di [hun kwI der]
  as quickly as possible yuè kuài yuè hǎo [yew-eh kwI yew-eh how]

quiet ānjìng [ahn-jing]

quite (*fairly*) xiāngdāng [syahng-dahng]

quote (*noun: for job etc.*) gūjià [goo-jyah]

R

radio shōuyīnjī [shoh-yin-jee]

rail: by rail zuò huǒchē [dzwor hwor-cher]

railway station huǒchē zhàn [hwor-cher jahn]　火车站

rain (*noun*) yǔ [yew]
　it's raining xià yǔ le [syah yew ler]

raincoat yǔyī [yew-yee]

rate of exchange duìhuàn lǜ [dway-hwahn lyew]　兑换

razor (*electric*) diàndòng tìhú dāo [dyen-doong tee-hoo dow]
　(*wet*) tìhú dāo

read (*aloud*) niàn, dú [nyen, doo]

　　could you read it out for me? qǐng ni bāng wǒ niàn yíxia, hǎo ma? [ching nee bahng wor nyen yee-syah how mah]

　　to read a book/newspaper kàn shū/bào [kahn shoo/bow]

ready (*goods, person*) zhǔnbèi hǎo le [joon-bay how ler]

real (*leather etc.*) zhēn de [jun der]

receipt shōujù [shoh-jyew]
　　can I have a receipt? nín néng gěi wo kāi ge shōujù ma? [neen nung gay wor kI ger shoh-jyew mah]

receive (*goods etc.*) shōudào [shoh-dow]

reception (*of hotel*) fúwùtái [foo-woo-tI]

red hóngsède [hoong-ser-der]

RED
The colour red is doubly important in China. Traditionally it was a lucky colour, associated with weddings and festivals like the New Year Festival. It also has echoes of luxury and the exotic. Added to this is the significance of red to the Communist Party. The national flag is red and red armbands, red characters for offical notices and red banners for special occasions can often be seen.

reduced price jiǎnjià [jyen-jyah]

reference number biānhào [byen-how]

registered mail guàhào yóujiàn [gwah-how yoh-jyen]

reliable (*person, company, machine*) kěkàode [ker-kow-der]

remember: I remember wǒ jìzhe [wor jee-jer]

rent (*verb: car etc.*) chūzū [choo-dzoo]

RENTING CARS

It is not usually possible to hire a car and drive it yourself in China. **Chūzū** means to hire the car and driver. So it is like taking a taxi in the West except that you can go further because it is cheaper.

repair xiūli [syew-lee]
   it needs repairing xūyao xiūli [syew-yow syew-lee]

repeat chóngfu [choong-foo]
   please repeat that qǐng zài shuō yíbiàn [ching dzI shwor yee-byen]

REPETITION *see* DUPLICATION.

reply (*noun*) huídá [hway-dah]
   we look forward to your reply wǒmen pànwàng nínde huíxìn [wor-mun pahn-wahng nee der hway-syeen]

representative (*noun: of company*) dàibiāo [dI-byow]

reserve (*seat*) dìngzuò [ding-dzwor]
   can I reserve a seat? wǒ kéyi dìng ge zuòwèi ma? [wor ker-yee ding ger dzwor-way mah]

rest (*siesta etc.*) xiūxi [syoh-syee]

restaurant (*small*) fànguǎnr [fahn-gwahnr]　饭馆
   (*big*) fàndiàn [fahn-dyen]

RESTAURANTS

China has a bewildering range of restaurants, and the vast majority of them are not at all used to catering for foreigners. Larger restaurants may be on two floors. The downstairs is quick turnover canteen-style. You choose your food from the board, buy your chits, and collect the food. Upstairs will have waiter service tables and a more extensive menu. And there will often be small rooms for private banquets and foreigners – with prices to match.

   Generally speaking, eating places can be divided into three groups:

1. The easiest for the foreign visitor are the restaurants in hotels, particularly the large modern Joint Venture hotels which have been specially designed for the foreign traveller. You can usually eat in their restaurants even if you are not a resident and the advantages are that you get a printed menu, including an English translation, and that the staff may understand some English. The disadvantage is that the food can be bland and uninspiring.

2. The second type of eating houses are the famous-name restaurants like the **Fāngshàn** [fahng-shahn], the **Quánjùdé** [chew-ahn-jyew-der] and the **Fēngzéyuán** [fung-dzer-yew-ahn] in Beijing. They are used to receiving groups of foreigners and have special rooms set aside upstairs or at the back. Many of these are renowned for particular dishes or a certain regional cuisine. If you wish to order a banquet you should book in advance and agree on a price per head or per table. The normal number of people for each table is eight to ten. So you can say:

> **wó xiǎng dìng liǎngzhuō cài bāge ren yìzhuō**
> [wor syahng ding lyahng-jwor tsI bah-ger run yee-jwor]
> I want to book two tables for eight people each

> **wo xiǎng yào gěi liǎng/sānge ren yùdìng**
> [wor syahng yow gay lyahng/sahn-ger run yoo-ding]
> I want to book a table for two/three

> **měi ren/yìzhuō yào duōshao qián?**
> [may run/yee-jwor yow dwor-show chyen]
> how much will it be per head/table?

3. For the visitor who knows little or no Chinese, the most difficult restaurants to cope with are the everyday eating places known as the 'masses restaurants'. These can be found everywhere, as the Chinese are fond of eating out, and they can vary from the sophisticated to the equivalent of a transport café. People are choosy about what they eat so the food is likely to be very good, but not necessarily to the taste of Westerners used to only a limited range of Chinese dishes. The main problem is that the menu, if there is one, is likely to be chalked up on a blackboard in Chinese and the chances are that the waitress will not speak English. This is obviously not going to put off the adventurous visitor. Examining what other people are eating and pointing to what you think you might like will probably get you

a meal and amuse the clientele at the same time. Unless you are particularly firm, there is a danger that you will be treated as a privileged guest rather than a customer and pushed to the front of the queue or served in a special room at the back. The easy way to solve this problem is to go with a Chinese friend.

Some useful phrases are:

no, no, he was first
bù, bù, tā zài wǒ qiántou
[boo boo tah dzI wor chyen-toh]

I'll try that
wǒ chángchang nèige cài
[wor chahng-chahng nay-ger tsI]

I'd like a typical local meal
wo xiǎng chángchang dāngdide fēngwèir
[wor syahng chahng-chahng dahng-dee-der fung-way-r]

return: a return ticket to . . . dào . . . de láihuí piào [dow . . . der lI-hway pyow]

Note that at the time of writing Chinese trains and long-distance buses do not have return tickets.

rice dàmǐ [dah-mee]
(*cooked*) mǐfàn [mee-fahn]

rice bowl fànwǎn [fahn-wahn]

rice field dàotián [dow-tyen]

rich (*person*) yǒuqián [yoh-chyen]

right (*correct*) duì [dway]
(*not left*) yòu(biānr) [yoh(byen-r)]
that's right duì le [dway ler]
all right (*I agree*) hǎo [how]
I'm all right, thanks (*not hurt etc.*) wǒ méi shìr, xièxie [wor may shur syeh-syeh]
that's all right (*doesn't matter*) méi guānxi [may gwahn-syee]
on the right zai yòubiānr [dzI yoh-byen-r]

rights (*to manufacture etc.*) quánlì [chyew-ahn-lee]

river hé [her]

There is also the word **jiāng**, which is used for some long rivers like the **Cháng jiāng** [chahng jyahng] or **Yangze**.

RMB Rénmínbì [run-min-bee]
See FOREIGN EXCHANGE CERTIFICATES.

road lù [loo]

room fángjiān [fahng-jyen]　房间
I'd like a room for two nights wo xiăng yào ge
fángjiān, zhù liăngge wănshang [wor syahng yow ger
fahng-jyen joo lyahng-ger wahng-shahng]
in my room zai wŏ fángjiān li

rubber (*material*) xiàngjiāo [syahng-jyow]
(*eraser*) xiàngpí [syahng-pee]

rubbish (*waste*) lājī [lah-jee]
(*nonsense*) fèihuà [fay-hwah]
(*poor-quality goods*) zhèi dōngxi zhìliàng bù xíng [jay
doong-syee jur-lyahng boo sying]

rude bù lĭmào [boo lee-mow]

Russia Éguó [er-gwor]

Russian (*adjective*) Éguó [er-gwor]
(*noun*) Éguo ren [er-gwor run]

S

sad (*person*) nánguò [nahn-gwor]
   (*news*) ràngrén nánguò de [rahng-run nahn-gwor der]

safe (*not dangerous*) ānquán [ahn-chyew-ahn]
   (*not in danger*) méishìr le [may-shur ler]

salad shālā [shah-lah] (*this is a borrowed word as salad is not part of Chinese cuisine*)

salary gōngzī [goong-dzur]

sale: for sale chūshòu [choo-shoh]

sales director yíngyèbù dǒngshì [ying-yeh-boo doong-shur]

salesman tuīxiāoyuán [tway-syow-yew-ahn]

salt yán [yen]

same xiāngtóng (de) [syahng-toong (de)]
   the same again, please qǐng zài lái yíge [ching dzI lI yee-ger]
   the same as him, please (*when ordering a meal*) gēn tāde yíyàng, xièxie [gun tah-der yee-yahng syeh-syeh]

sample (*noun: of goods, of work*) yàngpǐn [yahng-pin]

sandwich sānmíngzhì [sahn-ming-jur]

SANDWICHES
The sandwich is not really part of Chinese cuisine, but hotels used to catering for foreigners can produce them for a packed lunch on request. Increasingly popular in Western-style restaurants is the excellent club sandwich.

Saturday xīngqiliù [sying-chee-lyoh]

say shuō [shwor]
   what did he say? tā shuō shénme? [tah shwor shun-mah]
   he said ... tā shuō ...
   how do you say ... in Chinese? ... yòng Zhōngwén zěnme shuō? [yoong joong-wen dzun-mah shwor]
   how do you say it? (*pronounce*) zhèige zěnme niàn? [jay-ger dzun-mah nyen]

scarf wéijīn [way-jin]

schedule yuándìng jìndu [yew-ahn-ding jin-doo]
    work is on schedule gōngzuò ān yuándìng jìndu jìnxíng [goong-dzwor ahn yew-ahn-ding jin-doo jyen-sying]
    work is behind schedule gōngzuò méi ān yuándìng jìndu jìnxíng

school xuéxiào [syew-eh-syow]

SCHOOLS
Chinese schools are divided into primary (**xiǎoxué** [syow-syew-eh]) and secondary (**zhōngxué** [joong-syew-eh]) (*literally: middle schools*). Higher education institutions are classed as **dàxué** [dah-syew-eh] (universities) or **xuéyuan** [syew-eh-yew-ahn], which are specialist colleges.

scissors jiǎnzi [jyan-dzur]

Scotland Sūgélán [soo-ger-lahn]

scroll huàzhóu [hwah-joh]

sea hǎi [hI]
    by sea (*travel*) zuò chuán [dzwor chwahn]
    (*send*) hǎiyùn [hI yoon]

seal (*for printing name*) túzhāng [too-jahng]

SEALS
A 'seal' is a solid cylinder, usually of wood or stone, with the owner's name carved in one end. This can then be stamped on an ink pad and used in the same way that Westerners use a signature.

seat zuòwei [dzwor-way]

second (*adjective*) dì'èr [dee-er]
    See DATES.

second class (*travel*) èr dēng [er dung]
    See FIRST CLASS.

second-hand jiù(de) [jyoh(der)]
    second-hand bookshop jiù shūdiàn [jyoh shoo-dyen]

secretary mìshu [mee-shoo]
    my secretary wǒde mìshu [wor-der mee-shoo]
    his secretary tāde mìshu [tah-der mee-shoo]

see kànjian [kahn-jyen]
    can I see it? wǒ kéyi kànkan ma? [wor ker-yee kahn-kahn mah]

have you seen my colleague? nǐ jiànguo wǒde tóngshì ma? [nee jyen-gwor wor-der toong-shur mah]

I saw him a few minutes ago wǒ gāngcái kànjian tā le [wor gahng-tsI kahn-jyen tah ler]

let's wait and see wǒmen kànkan zài shuō [wor-mun kahn-kahn dzI shwor]

oh, I see ào, wǒ míngbai le [ow wor ming-bI ler]

sell mài [mI]

we sell ... wǒmen xiāoshòu ... [wor-mun syow-shoh]

Note that the word **mǎi** means exactly the opposite, i.e. 'to buy'. This is a very good example of how important tones are in speaking Chinese, because it is only the tone that makes the crucial difference in meaning when you say the word.

send sòng [soong]
(*by post*) jì [jee]
we'll send it out to you wǒmen huì jìgěi nín [wor-mun hway jee-gay neen]

September jiǔyuè [jyoh-yew-eh]

serious (*situation*) yánzhòng(de) [yen-joong(de)]
this is very serious wèntí hěn yánzhòng [wen-tee hun yen-joong]

sex (*male/female*) xìngbié [sying-byeh]

SEX

Modern China is extremely puritanical about sex. Until recently it was never discussed in public and there has been a great deal of ignorance among young people about the facts of life. Sex education has now been improved and the basic explanatory booklets published in the last few years are best-sellers. Sex outside marriage is officially frowned on and subject to severe social penalties ranging from criticism to actual imprisonment. Sex before marriage, particularly for the very young, can lead to disciplinary action by the work unit or a spell in a reformatory. Sexual relations between Chinese and foreigners are strongly discouraged. (It does happen, of course.) The authorities are even unhappy about mixed marriages.

The opening-up of China to the West has put many of these attitudes to the test. The press has recently highlighted a campaign against the import of pornographic books and video tapes, which has increased suddenly. Prostitution exists, although not at the level of before 1949. It is particularly prevalent in hotels used by visiting overseas Chinese in Guangzhou and Shanghai. The authorities take a very dim view of this and every attempt is being made to stamp it out.

shake yáo [yow]

shaking hands wòshǒu [wor-shoh]

SHAKING HANDS
The Western custom of shaking hands is generally understood, but the traditional Chinese gesture of **gōngshǒu** [goong-shoh] – cupping one hand in the other in front of the chest – is also used often and seems to be gaining in popularity again.

shame: that's a shame zhēn kěxī [jun ker-syee]

shampoo (*noun*) xǐfàjīng [syee-fah-jing]

sharp (*blade*) kuài [kwI]
    (*mentally*) hěn kuài [hun kwI]
    (*taste*) nóng [noong]

shave (*verb*) guāliän [gwah-lyen]

shaver diàndòng tìhú dāo [dyen-doong tee-hoo dow]

shaving soap tìhú yòng zào [tee-hoo yoong dzow]

she tā [tah]

SHE
The word for 'she', **tā**, is pronounced in exactly the same way as the word for 'he', but it is written with a different Chinese character. It can also mean 'her', depending on its position in the sentence:

>   **she is my colleague**
>   tā shi wǒ tóngshì

>   **I saw her**
>   wǒ kànjian tā le

ship chuán [chyew-ahn]
    by ship zuò chuán [dzwor chyew-ahn]

shipping company (*for freight*) hǎiyùn gōngsī [hI-yoon goong-sur]

shirt chènyī [chun-yee]

shoe xié [syeh]

shop (*noun*) shāngdiàn [shahng-dyen]
Note that when the word 'shop' comes after the name of the product it sells just use the Chinese word **diàn**. For example:

    shū diàn   bookshop
    xié diàn   shoeshop

short duǎn [dew-ahn]
    (*person*) ǎi [I]
    time is short shíjiān bùduō le [shur-jyen boo-dwor ler]

shoulder jiānbǎng [jyen-bahng]

show: can you show me? nǐ néng ràng wǒ kànkan ma? [nee nung rahng wor kahn-kahn mah]
    can you show me how it works? nǐ néng shìfàn yíxia ma? [nee nung shur-fahn yee-syah mah]

shower chōngzǎo [choong-dzow]
    (*of rain*) zhènyǔ [jun-yew]
    I'd like to take a shower wó xiǎng chōng ge zǎo [wor syahng choong ger dzow]

shut (*verb*) guān [gwahn]
    (*shop, office*) guānmén [gwahn mun]
    it's shut yǐjīng guānshang le [gwahn-shahng ler]
    (*shop, office*) yǐjīng guānmén le [yee-jing gwahn-mun ler]

Siberia Xībólìyà [syee-boh-lee-yah]

Siberian (*adjective*) Xībólìya(de) [syee-boh-lee-yah(der)]

sick (*ill*) yǒubìng [yoh-bing]
    I'm feeling sick (*like vomiting*) wǒ yóu diǎnr ěxīn [wor yoh dyenr er-syin]

side (*of box etc.*) biānr [byenr]
    (*of person*) páng [pahng]
    (*in game*) duì [dway]

sights lǚyóu diǎn [lyew-yoh dyen]
    the sights of . . . de lǚyóu diǎn . . .

sign (*verb: document*) qiānzì [chyen-dzur]
    please sign here qǐng zai zhèr qiān [ching dzI jer chyen]
    where do I sign? zai nǎr qiān? [dzI nahr chyen]

signature qiānzì [chyen-dzur]

silk sīchóu [sur-choh]

Silk Road sīchóu zhī lù [sur-choh jur loo]

silver yín(zi) [yin(dzur)]

similar xiāngjìn de [syahng-jin der]
  it's similar but not the same hěn xiāngjìn què bù xiāngtóng [hun syahng-jin chyew-eh boo syahng-toong]

since: since our last meeting zìcóng wǒmen shàngci jiànmiàn yǐlái [dzur-tsoong wor-mun shahng-tsur jyen-myen yee-lI]
  since last year zìcóng qùnián yǐlái [dzur-tsoong chyew-nyen yee-lI]

sing chànggē [chahng-ger]

Singapore Xīnjiāpō [syin-jyah-poh]

single: I'm single wǒ shi dānshēn [wor shur dahn-shun]

single room dānrén jiān [dahn-run jyen]

single ticket (dānchéng) piào [dahn-chung pyow]
  See **return**.

sir xiānsheng [syen-shung]
  See ADDRESSING PEOPLE.

sister jiěmèi [jyeh-may]
  (*elder*) jiějie [jyeh-jyeh]
  (*younger*) mèimei [may-may]

sit zuò [dzwor]
  can I sit here? wǒ kéyi zuò zhèr ma? [wor ker-yee dzwor jer mah]
  please sit down qǐng zuò [ching dzwor]

SITTING

At meetings and meals the Chinese sit around a table as in the West. Seating will usually be arranged by the host organization with the more senior at the centre of a long table.

More informally, people often squat on their heels rather than sit – and they do this for meals as well. Often in China (at railway stations, bus stations, on the pavement or outside their houses in the country) you will see people squatting on their heels to rest or gossip. This produced no problems for women in the days when trousers were worn all the time. Since skirts have become popular, elaborate and ingenious ways of folding them have been devised to enable women to squat with decency.

size (*of clothing*) chǐcùn [chur-tsoon]

skin (*human*) pífu [pee-foo]
(*animal*) pí

skirt qúnzi [chyewn-dzur]

SKIRTS
Skirts or dresses are universal summer wear for younger women although some older women still prefer trousers.

sky tiān [tyen]

sleep (*verb*) shuìjiào [shway-jyow]
I need some sleep wǒ xūyào shuì huǐr [wor syew-yow shway hway-r]
did you sleep well? nǐ shuì de hǎo ma? [nee shway der how mah]

slow màn [mahn]
very slowly hěn màn [hun mahn]

small xiǎo [syow]

smell (*noun*) wèir [way-r]

smile (*noun*) wēixiào [way-syow]

SMILES
A smile need not always mean someone is pleased: the Chinese also smile with embarrassment.

smoke: do you smoke? (*offering cigarette*) nín chōuyān ma? [neen choh-yen mah]
may I smoke? wǒ kéyi chōuyān ma? [wor ker-yee choh-yen mah]

SMOKING
China often seems to be a society of chain-smokers, although the offenders are mostly men. Cigarettes, which in China seem weaker and less tarry than their Western equivalents, are handed out with the tea at meetings, so, if you don't smoke, it is useful to be able to say:

wǒ bú huì chōuyān [wor boo hway choh-yen]
I don't smoke

Smoking can also spoil a long train journey for non-smokers as there are no non-smoking compartments. Recently a campaign against smoking has begun. This was apparently impossible while Chairman Mao was alive as he was an extremely heavy smoker.

snow (*noun*) xuě [syew-eh]
  (*verb*) xià xuě [syah syew-eh]

so zhème [jun-mah]
  not so fast/loud, please qǐng bié zhème kuài/dàshēng
  [ching byeh jun-mah kwI/dah-shung]
  it's so warm zhēn nuǎnhuo [jun nwahn-hwor]

soap féizào [fay-dzow]

socialism shèhuì zhǔyì [sher-hway joo-yee]

sock duǎnwà [dwahn-wah]

soft drink qìshuǐr [chee-shwayr]

software ruǎnjiàn [rwahn-jyen]

sole rights zhuānyǒu quán [jwahn-yoh chyew-ahn]

some yìxiē [yee-syeh]
  some of our products wǒmende yìxiē chǎnpǐn [wor-mun-der yee-syeh chahn-pin]

SOME

Although 'some' by itself can be translated by **yìxiē**, when it is put into a phrase the translation can vary according to context:

  some of us
  wómen yǒude ren
  [wor-mun yoh-der run]

  some are cheap, some are expensive
  yǒde piányi, yǒde guì
  [yoh-der pyen-yee yoh-der gway]

  may I have some tea?
  qǐng lái diǎnr chá, hǎo ma?
  [ching lI dyenr chah how ma]
  (*literally: please come a bit tea all right?*)

Often the word 'some' is simply dropped in the translation:

  do you have some matches/paper?
  ní yǒu huǒchái/zhǐ ma?
  [nee yoh hwor-chee/jur ma]
  (*literally: you have matches/paper?*)

somebody yǒurén [yoh-run]
  somebody is waiting/looking for you
  yǒurén děng/zhǎo ni
  [yoh-run dung/jow ni]
  (*literally: have person wait for/look for you*)
  I am waiting for/looking for somebody
  wǒ zai děng/zhǎo rén

[wor dzI dung/jow run]
(*literally: I wait for/look for person*)

something
There are various ways of expressing 'something', depending on context:

> **something to drink/eat?**
> hē/chī diănr shénme ba?
> [her/chee dyenr shun-mah bah]
> (*literally: drink/eat a bit what?*)

> **I have got something to give you**
> wó xiăng sòng ní diănr dōngxi
> [wor syahng soong ni dyenr doong-syee]
> (*literally: I want give you a bit thing*)

sometimes yŏushíhòu [yoh-shur-hoh]

somewhere (*at a certain place*) mŏudì [moh-dee]
> **I am looking for somewhere to stay/eat** wó xiang zhăo ge dìfang zhù/chīfàn [wor syahng jI ger dee-fahng joo/chur-fahn]

son érzi [er-dzur]

soon yìhuĭr [yee-hway-r]
> **we'll be back soon** wŏmen yìhuĭr jiù huílai [wor-mun yee-hway-r jyoh hway-lI]
> **as soon as possible** yuè kuài yuè hăo [yew-eh kwI yew-eh how]

sorry duìbuqĭ [dway-boo-chee]
> **I'm very sorry** zhēn duìbuqĭ [jun dway-boo-chee]

sort (*type*) zhŏng [joong]
> **a different sort of ...** lìngwài yìzhŏng ... [ling-wI yee-joong]

soup tāng [tahng]

south nán [nahn]
> **in the south** nánfāng [nahn-fahng]

souvenir jìniànpĭn [jee-nyen-pin]
> **as a souvenir** zuòwei jìniàn [dzwor-way jee-nyen]

Soviet Union Sūlián [soo-lyen]

soy sauce jiàngyóu [jyahng-yoh]

soya bean dàdòu [dah-doh]

speak jiăng [jyahng]
> **do you speak English?** nín huì jiăng Yīngyŭ ma? [neen hway jyahng ying-yew mah]
> **may I speak English?** wŏ kéyi jiăng Yīngyŭ ma? [wor ker-yee jyahng ying-yew mah]

I don't speak ... wŏ búhuì jiăng ... [wor boo-hway jyahng]

can I speak to ...? *(on telephone)* máfan nín zhăo yíxia ... , hăo ma? [mah-fahn neen jow yee-syah ... how mah]

I wish I could speak Chinese wŏ yào huì jiăng Zhōngwén jiù hăole [wor yow hway jyahng joong-wun jyoh how-ler]

special tèbié(de) [ter-byeh(der)]

speed *(noun)* sùdu [soo-doo]

we'll try to speed things up wŏmen yào jiākuài diănr sùdu [wor-mun yow jyah-kwI dyenr soo-doo]

SPITTING

Spitting is still very common everywhere in China despite regular campaigns to discourage the habit. Spittoons are still visible in the more traditional hotels and meeting rooms.

spoon tiáogĕng [tyow-gung]

spring *(season)* chūntian [choon-tyen]

in the spring chūntian

SPRING FESTIVAL *see* NEW YEAR.

stairs lóutī [loh-tee]

stamp yóupiào [yoh-pyow]

two stamps for Great Britain please qĭng mài wo liăngzhāng dào Yīngguo de yóupiào [ching mI wor lyahng-jahng dow ying-gwor der yoh-pyow]

stand *(noun: at trade fair etc.)* zhăntái [jahn-tI]

at our stand zai wŏmende zhăntái [dzI wor-mun-der jahn-tI]

at your stand zai nĭmende zhăntái [dzI nee-mun-der jahn-tI]

Standard Chinese pŭtōnghuà [poo-toong-hwah]

This used to be known as Mandarin, but that is now an obsolete word and unpopular with the Chinese.

start *(verb)* kāishī [kI-shur]

starting from next month cóng xiàge yuè kāishī [tsoong syah-ger yew-eh kI-shur]

station zhàn [jahn]　站

(railways) huŏchē zhàn [hwor-cher jahn]

(bus) qìchē zŏngzhàn [chee-cher dzoong-jahn]

stay: I'm staying at ... wŏ zhù zai ... [wor joo dzI]

steal tōu [toh]
    my suitcase has been stolen wǒde xiāngzi gěi tōu le
    [wor-der syahng-dzur gay toh ler]

STEALING
Theft is far from unknown in China and, as consumer durables become more widely available, it is on the increase. There are occasionally reports in the press about major robberies and those are dealt with severely.

    Western visitors are very unlikely to be robbed, as this would be regarded as bringing great shame on the nation. There are countless stories about foreigners being pursued halfway across China by a watermelon or an empty medicine bottle that they tried to throw away. Generally hotel staff are extremely honest in their dealings with foreigners, but little things can disappear, so it is unwise to take no precautions.

steamed roll huājuǎnr [hwah-jew-ahnr]

sterling (*currency*) yīngbàng [ying-bahng]

sticking plaster zhíxuě gāobù [jee-syew-eh gow-boo]

still hái(shi) [hI(shur)]
    it's still not right háishi bú duì [hI-shur boo dway]

stomach wèi [way]

stomach-ache wèiténg [way-tung]

stop (*verb*) tíng [ting]
    could you stop here, please? (*to taxi driver etc.*) qǐng nín zai zhèr tíngchē, hǎo ma? [ching neen dzI jer ting-cher how mah]
    does this train stop at ...? zhèitang chē zai ... tíng ma? [jay-tahng cher dzI ... ting mah]

straight zhíde [jur-der]
    straight on yìzhí zǒu [yee-jur dzoh]

strange qíguài de [chee-gwI der]

stranger: I'm a stranger here wǒ dìyī cì lái zhèr [wor dee-yee tsur lI jer]

street jiē(dào) [jyeh(dow)]
    the next street on the left zuǒbiānr di'èr tiáo jiē [dzwor-byenr dee-er tyow jyeh]
    what street is it on? zai něi tiáo jiē? [dzI nay tyow jyeh]
    could you write the street name down? máfan nín bǎ zhèi tiáo jiē de míngzi xiě xiàlai, hǎo ma? [mah-fahn

neen bah jay tyow jyeh der ming-dzur syeh syah-lI how mah]

strike (*noun*) bàgōng [bah-goong]

string shéngzi [shung-dzur]

strong (*material*) jiēshi [jyeh-shur]
(*taste, drink*) nóng [noong]

student xuésheng [syew-eh-shung]

stupid bèn [bun]

successful chénggōng [chung-goong]
here's to a successful relationship! (*in a toast*) wèi wŏmende chénggōng hézuò, gānbēi! [way wor-mun-der chung-goong her-dzwor gahn-bay]

suddenly tūrán [too-rahn]

sugar táng [tahng]

suit (*noun: clothing*) tàozhuāng [tow-jwahng]

suitcase shŏutíxiāng [shoh-tee-syahng]

summer xiàtian [syah-tyen]
in the summer xiàtian

sun tàiyang [tI-yahng]

sun glasses tàiyang jìng [tI-yahng jing]

sunburnt: I've got sunburnt wŏ shàibào pí le [wor shI-bow pee ler]

Sunday xīngqitiān [sying-chee-tyen]

suntan lotion fángshài jì [fahng-shI jee]

supper wănfàn [wahn-fahn]

SUPPER *see* DINNER.

supplier chăngshāng [chahng-shahng]

supply (*verb*) tígōng [tee-goong]

sure: I'm sure wó gan kěndìng [wor gahn kun-ding]
I'm not sure wŏ bù gan kěndìng
are you sure? zhēnde ma? [jun-der mah]

surname xìng [sying]

SURNAMES

Chinese surnames (**xìng**), which always come before the given name, are nearly all of one syllable. **Sīmă** [sur-ma] and **Ōuyáng** [oh-yahng] are the only fairly common two-syllable names. Recent research has shown that the most common surname is **Lĭ** (7.9 per cent of the Han Chinese population), closely followed by **Wáng** [wahng] (7.4 per cent) and **Zhāng** [jahng] (7.1 per cent). Sixteen other surnames are very common (each borne by over 1 per cent of the Han population). These are:

Liú [lyoh], **Chén** [chun], **Yáng** [yahng], **Zhào** [jow], **Huáng** [hwahng], **Zhōu** [joh], **Wú** [woo], **Xú** [syew], **Sūn** [soon], **Hú** [hoo], **Zhū** [joo], **Gāo** [gow], **Lín** [lin], **Hé** [her], **Guō** [gwor] and **Mǎ** [mah].

If you add eighty-one more common surnames, this brings the total up to a hundred and accounts for 87 per cent of the population. The ordinary people of China have been referred to for centuries as the **láobǎixìng**, the old hundred surnames. The real number in use at present (common and uncommon) is far greater than this and some estimates put it as high as 3,000.

To ask someone's surname you can ask them:

> **nǐ xìng shénme?**
> [nee sying shun-mah]

or **nǐ xìng . . . ?**

The most polite way is to ask:

> **nín guìxìng?**
> [neen gway-sying]
> what is your honoured surname?

or **xiānsheng guìxìng?**
> [syen-shung gway-sying]
> what is sir's honoured surname?

These are thought to be rather too old-fashioned and feudal for egalitarian socialist China, but are often used to foreigners and by country people talking to officials.

swearword zāngzìr [dzahng-dzur]

SWEARWORDS

Chinese is as rich in obscenities and swearwords as any other highly developed language and culture, but no one should attempt to use them without living in China for a long time and getting used to the usage and nuances.

Some of the more refined swearwords that are fairly safe to use are:

> **tāmāde!**
> [tah-mah-der]
> hell!

shénjīngbìng!
[shun-jing-bing]
crazy!, not right in the head!

bèndàn!
[bun-dahn]
bloody idiot!

húndàn!
[hoon-dahn]
shit!, bastard!

fèihuà!
[fay-hwah]
rubbish!

fàngpì!
[fahng-pee]
crap!

swim yóuyǒng [yoh-yoong]

swimming pool yóuyǒng chí [yoh-yoong chur]

switch (*light switch, on machine etc.*) kāiguān [kI-gwahn]

T

table zhuōzi [jwor-dzur]

Taiwan Táiwān [tI-wahn]

Taiwanese (*adjective*) Táiwān(de) [tI-wahn(der)]
(*noun*) Táiwān ren [tI-wahn run]

take ná [nah]
I'll take it (*buy*) wó mǎixià le [wor mI-syah ler]
how long does it take? (*journey, job*) yào duōcháng
shíjiān? [yow dwar-chahng shur-jyen]

talk tánhuà [tahn-hwah]
can I talk to ...? wǒ néng gēn ... tántan ma? [wor
nung gun ... tahn-tahn mah]

tall gāo [gow]

Taoism Dàojiào [dow-jyow]

tap shuǐlóng tóu [shway-loong toh]
(*literally: water dragon head*)

tape (*for tape-recorder*) cídài [tsur-dI]

tape-recorder lùyīnjī [loo-yin-jee]

taxi chūzū qìchē [choo-dzoo chee-cher] 出租汽车

TAXIS
Taxis (**chūzū qìchē**) are run by taxi companies,
which grow in number every year. Taxis are often
based at the big hotels and can be booked there or at
the offices of China Travel – **Lǚxíngshè**. In Guangzhou, you can hail a taxi at the roadside, and it is
now becoming more common to do this in Beijing.
Some taxis in Guangzhou advertise that they take
RMB, so they are available to local Chinese. Most
only accept Foreign Exchange Certificates. Using a
taxi is a quick way to get through the traffic of
Beijing or one of the other large cities. It is
expensive in comparison with bus travel but is still
relatively cheap by Western standards.
   It can be quite a weird experience being whisked
through Beijing dusk in a shiny Toyota with the
stereo playing the latest US or Japanese chart hits
while China goes about at its own pace on bikes or
in buses. If you want to be cut off from Chinese

reality or don't mind and can afford it, you can travel everywhere like this.

tea chá [chah]   茶
a cup of tea yìbēi chá [yee-bay chah]

TEA

Tea is one of China's gifts to the world. Everybody drinks it everywhere and it has an important social function. When you visit a factory or an office or a school, you will be sat down and given tea, almost always green tea, as a welcome. It is not necessary to finish the tea but you should take at least a few sips.

Nearly all Chinese carry their own mug and tea leaves with them when travelling, especially on trains, where the attendant passes around frequently with a giant kettle. And in some of the older teahouses you are also expected to bring your own tea.

There are two main categories of Chinese tea:

> **lǜ chá**
> [lyew chah]
> green tea

which is by far the commonest especially in north China and

> **hóng chá**
> [hoong chah]
> red tea

which is drunk more often in the south.

'Red' tea is actually black but looks reddish when you brew it. It is similar to the Indian tea drunk in Europe. Chinese tea is drunk freshly brewed and without milk or sugar, and is often served with the leaves still in it. It is ready to drink when the leaves have sunk to the bottom of the mug or glass.

There are also scented teas (**huāchá** [hwah-chah]) – which are green teas with flower petals added. The most popular of these is jasmine tea (**mòlihuā chá** [moh-lee-hwah chah]). Tea enthusiasts frown on scented teas and will only drink pure green teas.

If you really must have milk in your tea, say:

> **yóu dianr nǎi ma?**
> [yoh dyenr nI mah]
> is there a litle milk?

and if sugar is crucial you can say:

> **yóu dianr táng ma?**
> [yoh dyenr tahng mah]

is there a little sugar?

You are unlikely to be served milk and sugar except in the Western restaurants of tourist hotels.

Here is some useful tea-drinking vocabulary:

teacup
chábēi
[chah-bay]

teahouse
cháguǎnr, cháshì
[chah-gwahnr, chah-shur]

teapot
cháhú
[chah-hoo]

tea set
chájù
[chah-jyew]

Teas are produced in many areas of south China, and among the best known are the 'Dragon Well' tea, Lóngjǐn from Zhejiang, the **Oolong** teas, **Wūlóng chá**, from Fujian and the red **Qímén chá** or **Keemun** tea (also known as **Qíhóng**) from Anhui. Chinese travelling through tea-producing areas will look out for fine varieties to take home, and the wise foreign visitor does the same. **Wūlóng chá** has become even more popular recently as it has a reputation for helping people to lose weight!

In case you are wondering, the Chinese word for tea is in fact the origin of our slang word 'char'.

teacher lǎoshī [low-shur]

telegram diànbào [dyen-bow]

telephone (*noun*) diànhuà [dyen-hwah]
(*verb*) dǎ diànhuà
  can I use your telephone? jiè nín diànhuà yòng yíxia, hǎo ma? [jyeh neen dyen-hwah yoong yee-syah how mah]
  is there a telephone nearby? fùjìn yǒu diànhuà ma? [foo-jin yoh dyen-hwah mah]

telephone directory diànhuà hàomǎ bù [dyen-hwah how-mah boo]

TELEPHONING

Some of the things you might want to say on the telephone are:

  can I speak to ...?
  máfan nín zhǎo yíxia ... hǎo ma?

[mah-fahn neen jow yee-syah . . . how mah]

this is . . .
wǒ shi . . .
[wor shur]

I'll call back later
wǒ guò yìhuǐr zài dǎ ba
[wor gwor yee-hway-r dzI dah bah]

when will he be back?
tā shénme shíhou néng huílai?
[tah shun-mah shur-hoh nung hway-lI]

please say Mr . . . called
máfan nín zhuǎngào yíxia, yǒu ge xìng . . . de
láiguo diànhuà, hǎo ma
[mah-fahn neen jwahn-gow yee-syah, yoh ger
sying . . . der lI-gwor dyen-hwah how mah]

Some of things that you might hear on the telephone are:

wái
[way]
hello

ní zhǎo shéi?
[nee jow shay]
who do you want to speak to?

tā bú zài
[tah boo dzI]
he's not here

yào wǒ zhuǎngào shénme ma?
[yow wor jwahng-gow shun-mah mah]
can I take a message?

qǐng gàosu wǒ nínde diànhuà hǎo ma?
[ching gow-soo wor neen-der dyen-hwah how
mah]
please give me your phone number

television diànshì [dyen-shur]

TELEVISION
The Chinese are avid watchers of programmes for
teaching foreign languages, news and sport. A great
many series from Britain and the USA are now
being bought, but Chinese television still broadcasts
mainly local plays, operas and animated features.

telex diànchuán [dyen-chwahn]

temperature (*fever*) fāshāo [fah-show]

temple (*Buddhist*) sì [sur]
  (*Taoist*) miào [myow]

Temple of Heaven Tiāntán [tyen-tahn]

terms (*of contract*) tiáokuǎn [tyow-kwahn]

terrible tài zāogāo le [tI dzow-gow ler]

than bǐ [bee]
  it's better than this one nèige bǐ zhèige hǎo yìxie
  [nay-ger bee jay-ger how yee-syeh]
  See COMPARISON.

thank you xièxie [syeh-syeh]
  thank you very much duōxiè [dwor-syeh]
  no, thank you xièxie, wǒ bú yào [syeh-syeh wor boo
  yow]

THANK YOU

The official word for thank you is **xièxie**, but
overusing it sounds formal and therefore rather
foreign. For example, at table Chinese might just say
hǎo [how].

If someone has done you a specific service, or if
you want to say 'thank you' to your hosts for having
taken you sightseeing or to the airport etc., then you
can say:

  máfan nǐ le
  [mah-fahn nee ler]

which literally means:

  I have caused you some trouble

If you say 'thank you' to someone, they are likely to
reply:

  bié kèqi
  [byeh ker-chee]
  don't be so polite

or: **méi shénme**
  [may shun-mah]
  it was nothing, you're welcome

that nà [nah]
  what is that? nà shi shénme? [nah shur shun-mah]
  that's for you nà shi géi nǐ de [nah shur gay nee der]

THAT

When 'that' is followed by classifiers or numerals it
is translated in Chinese by **nèi** [nay]:

  that man
  nèige rén

[nay-ger run]
that flight
nèitàng fēijī
[nay-tahng fay-jee]
can I have that one?
wŏ yào nèige, xíng ma?
[wor yow nay-ger sying mah]
See CLASSIFIERS.

the

There are no words in Chinese corresponding to the definite article 'the'. So, for example, **shū** can mean either 'a book', 'books', 'the book' or 'the books'.

If you want to emphasize that you are talking about an object that has been mentioned before, you can use the word **nà** [nah] or **nèi** [nay] (that)

the book (i.e. that we have discussed already)
nèi bĕn shū
[nay bun shoo]

theatre jùyuàn [jyew-yew-ahn]

their, theirs tāmende [tah-mun-der]
Tāmende can mean either 'their' or 'theirs':

those are their suitcases
zhèixie shi tāmende xíngli
[jay-syeh shur tah-mun-der sying-lee]

those are theirs
zhèixie shi tāmende

them tāmen [tah-mun]
Note that **tāmen** can also mean 'they' depending on context:

I know them
wŏ rènshi tāmen
[wor run-shur tah-mun]

they know me
tāmen rènshi wŏ

then (*afterwards*) ránhòu [rahn-hoh]
(*at that time*) nèige shíhou [nay-ger shur-hoh]

there nàr [nahr]
there is ... yŏu ... [yoh]
there are ... yŏu ...
is there ...? yŏu ... ma? [yoh ... mah]
are there ...? yŏu ... ma?
there isn't/aren't ... méi yŏu ... [may yoh]

these zhèixiē [jay-syeh]
See CLASSIFIERS.

they tāmen [tah-mun]
Note that **tāmen** can also mean 'them' depending on context.

thick (*not thin*) hòu [hoh]

thin báo [bow]

thing (*matter*) shìr [shur]
(*object*) dōngxi [doong-syee]

think xiǎng [syahng]
what do you think? ní zěnme xiǎng? [nee dzun-mah syahng]
I think so wóxiǎng shi zhèiyang [wor syahng shur jay-ahng]
I don't think so wǒ bù zhèiyang xiǎng
we'll have to think about it wǒmen děi kǎolǜ kǎolü [wor-mun day kow-lyew kow-lyew]

third class sānděng [sahn-dung]
See FIRST CLASS.

thirsty kě [ker]
I'm very thirsty wó hén kě [wor hun ker]

this zhè [jer]
what is this? zhè shi shénme? [jer shur shun-mah]
is this yours? zhè shi nǐde ma? [jer shur nee-der mah]

THIS
When 'this' is followed by classifiers or numerals it is translated in Chinese by **zhèi** [jay]:
this man
zhèige rén
[jay-ger run]
this flight
zhèitàng fēijī
[jay-tahng fay-jee]
can I have this one?
wǒ yào zhèige, xíng ma?
[wor yow jay-ger sying mah]
this is Mr MacDonald (*introducing him*)
zhèiwèi shi Màiketángnà xiānsheng
[jay-way shur MacDonald syen-shung]
See CLASSIFIERS.

those nèixie [nay-syeh]
See CLASSIFIERS.

throat sǎngzi [sahng-dzur]

through tōngguò [toong-gwor]
  through Shanghai jīngguò Shànghǎi [jing-gwor shahng-hI]

Thursday xīngqīsì [sying-chee-sur]

ticket (*for flight, train, bus, theatre*) piào [pyow]

tie (*clothing*) lǐngdài [ling-dI]

tight (*schedule*) jǐn [jin]
  (*fit, clothes*) xiǎo [syow]

tights liánkùwà [lyen-koo-wah]

time shíjiān [shur-jyen]
  there's not much time méi yǒu duōshao shíjiān le [may yoh doh-show shur-jyen ler]
  we've plenty of time wǒmen háiyǒu hěnduō shíjiān [wor-mun hI-yoh hun-doh shur-jyen]
  last time shàng yícì [shahng yee-tsur]
  next time xià yícì [syah yee-tsur]

TIME TELLING

The normal way of asking the time is:

  what's the time?
  xiànzai jí diǎn le?
  [syen-dzI jee dyen ler]
  (*literally: now how many hours?*)

To answer that it is, for example, 3 o'clock, you just replace the **jǐ** with the number **sān**, and similarly for all other times:

  (it is) 3/4 o'clock
  (xiànzai) sāndiǎn/sìdiǎn le
  [(syen-dzI) sahn-dyen/sur-dyen ler]

Other commonly used words in telling the time are:

  half
  bàn
  [bahn]

  quarter past
  yíkè
  [yee-ker]

  quarter to
  chā yíkè
  [chah yee-ker]

  minutes
  fēn
  [fun]

Here are some examples:

3.00   sāndiǎn

3.10	sāndiǎn shífēn
3.15	sāndiǎn yíkè
3.30	sāndiǎn bàn
3.40	sāndiǎn sìshí
3.45	chā yíkè sìdiǎn
	or sāndiǎn sìshíwǔ

To be more precise about the part of the day, you can put **shàngwǔ** [shahng-woo] for morning, **xiàwǔ** [syah-woo] for afternoon or **wǎnshang** [wahn-shahng] for evening (after 6 p.m.) before the times:

7.00 a.m.	shàngwǔ qīdiǎn
4.35 p.m.	xiàwǔ sìdiǎn sānshíwǔ
6.30 p.m.	wǎnshang liùdiǎn bàn

Noon is **zhōngwǔ** [joong-woo] and midnight is **bànyè** [bahn-yeh].
    The 24-hour clock is used for timetables.

timetable (*for travel*) shíkèbiǎo [shur-ker-byow]

tip (*to waiter etc.*) xiǎo fèi [syow-fay]

TIPPING
In China tipping is officially regarded as a feudal remnant and is seen as an insult as it implies that waiters and other service personnel are not paid enough. Foreigners visiting China have started to tip in the larger hotels and the service personnel often like this – but the government has issued stern warnings that tips should not be accepted. Smiles and words of thanks are always appreciated.

tired lèi [lay]
    I'm tired wǒ lèi le [wor lay ler]

tissues zhǐjīn [jur-jeen]

TISSUES
Cotton handkerchiefs are much more commonly used than tissues in China. They are, unlike tissues, widely available and cheap. You will find that many Chinese just use their fingers to wipe their nose.

to dào [dow]
    to London dào Lúndūn [dow loon-doon]
    to Peace Hotel, please qǐng dào Hépíng fàndiàn [ching dow her-ping fahn-dyen]

TO

It is quite common to omit the word for 'to' in Chinese and just to use the name of a place after the word for 'go':

> **tomorrow I'm going to . . .**
> wǒ míngtian qù . . .
> [wor ming-tyen chyew]
> (*literally: I tomorrow go . . .*)

toast (*bread*) kǎo miànbāo [kow myen-bow]
(*drinking*) zhùjiǔ [joo-jyoh]

TOASTS

The commonest Chinese toast is:

> **gānbēi**
> [gahn-bay]
> cheers

You can also say:

> **zhù nǐ jiànkāng!**
> [joo nee jyen-kahng]
> your very good health!

tobacco yānyè [yen-yeh]

today jīntian [jin-tyen]

toe jiáozhǐtou [jyow-zhur-toh]

together yìqǐ [yee-chee]
  can we pay together? wǒmen kéyi yìqǐ fù ma? [wor-mun ker-yee yee-chee foo mah]

toilet cèsuǒ [tser-swor]
  can I use your toilet? wǒ néng yòng yíxia nínde cèsuǒ ma? [wor nung yoong yee-syah neen-der tsur-swor mah]

toilet paper wèishēngzhǐ
  (*literally: hygiene paper*) [way-shuhng-jee]

TOILETS 厕所

Chinese toilets are internationally notorious and with some justification. Only toilets in hotels which cater for foreigners are just as you would expect to find in Western hotels – and finicky foreigners try never to use any others. Public toilets in cities are found in every alleyway as many houses still have none of their own. They are marked with:

男厕所

> **nán cèsuǒ**
> [nahn tser-swor]

gents

and 女厕所

nǚ cèsuǒ
[nyew tser-swor]
ladies

These tend to be the first Chinese characters that foreigners learn to recognize, but it is immediately obvious even to the untrained nose what they are. There are no seats, just a hole in the floor. The authorities are aware of the poor image of China that these toilets convey and a programme to improve them has been launched. A sparkling new public convenience in the centre of Nanjing attracted a great deal of attention from the locals.

All excrement, human and animal, is used as fertilizer and the night-soil carriers pulling their 'honey-carts' out towards the field are a familiar sight in Chinese cities. Their traditional low status was given a boost in the 1960s when they became the subject of a popular song: 'The Nightsoil Collectors are Coming Down the Mountain'.

In the countryside the link between toilets and agriculture is even more direct and villages often just have earth closets. If you want to use toilet paper you will have to bring your own. If you want privacy, you will have to wait till you get back to your hotel.

tomorrow míngtian [ming-tyen]
    tomorrow morning míngtian zǎoshang [ming-tyen dzow-shahng]
    tomorrow evening míngtian wǎnshang [ming-tyen wahn-shahng]
    the day after tomorrow hòutian [hoh-tyen]

ton dūn [doon]

TONES

Chinese, like Vietnamese, Thai, Lao and other languages of East and South East Asia, is usually described as a tonal language. The tone or pitch of the voice varies within a syllable. In Western languages this might just change the emphasis. In Chinese it can change the meaning completely and the tones of a word have to be learned as an integral part of that word.

Tone patterns are complex, but words in Standard Chinese are assigned to one of four tones, represented in the Pinyin romanization by marks above each syllable.

The four tones in which the syllable **ma** [mah] can be pronounced in Standard Chinese, **pǔtōnghuà**, are represented by:

mā   má   mǎ   mà

These are known as first, second, third and fourth tones.

In **mā**, which has a basic meaning of 'mother' the pitch of the voice starts high and stays roughly level, although this does not mean that a man with a bass voice has to start off with a squeak.

In **má**, which means 'hemp', the voice starts low and rises.

In **mǎ**, which means 'horse', the voice drops and rises again.

In **mà**, to scold or curse, the voice starts high and drops.

Looking at the different meanings that **ma** can have, it is obvious that the tone is crucial. An even clearer example is the difference between the two words:

       mǎi [mI]   to buy
and   **mài**   to sell

Clearly, money could be lost in a mistake in tones. Although Chinese ears are attuned to these tone differences, they have to make allowances, as even native **pǔtōnghuà** speakers from different areas have different tone patterns. In practice, words like **mā** and **mǎ** would never be used in a way that could cause confusion. And in written Chinese there would be no confusion since these words are represented by different characters. For 'mother', Chinese would say **māma** or **mǔqin**, thereby avoiding confusion. In some areas the words for 10 and 4 are distinguishable only by tone **sí** (standard pronunciation **shí**) and **sì** and it is quite common for people to hold up fingers to indicate which they mean.

Textbooks and dictionaries emphasize the tones of individual syllables and words and this is where the beginner must start. In more fluent speech, what is important is the tone pattern of the whole sentence and that only comes with long experience of listening and imitating.

Some syllables have no tones. And one common modification in tonal patterns is for a third tone to be changed to a second tone when immediately followed by another third tone, for example:

wŏ xiăng

becomes

wó xiăng

Other forms of Chinese have even more complicated tonal patterns than Standard Chinese. Cantonese, for example, has six tones.

tongue shétou [sher-toh]

tonight jīntian wănshang [jin-tyen wahn-shahng]

too (*excessively*) tài [tI]
(*also*) yĕ [yeh]
it's too expensive tài guìle [tI gway-ler]

TOO

There is no one phrase for 'me too' in Chinese. The verb to which the speaker is referring has to be repeated (this is similar to the way Chinese expresses 'no' in response to a question – *see* NEGATIVES). Here are some examples of how to say 'me too' in Chinese:

I want to go
wó xiăng qù
[wor syahng chyew]

me too
wŏ yé xiăng qù
[wor yeh syahng chyew]
(*literally: I want to go too*)

I'd like a beer
wŏ yào píjiŭ
[wor yow pee-jyoh]

me too
wó yĕ yào píjiŭ
[wor yeh yow pee-jyoh]
(*literally: I'd like a beer too*)

tooth yá [yah]

toothache yáténg [yah-tung]

toothbrush yáshuā [yah-shwah]

toothpaste yágāo [yah-gow]

top (*of box etc.*) gàir [gIr]

torch shŏudiàntŏng [shoh-dyen-toong]

total (*noun*) zŏnggòng [dzoong-goong]

tour (*noun*) lǚxíng [lyew-sying]

tourist lǚyóu zhĕ [lyew-yoh jur]

towel máojīn [mow-jin]

TOWELS
Chinese nearly always carry a small hand towel, especially when travelling, constantly wiping themselves with it to keep clean and dry. In some parts of north China you will see people with a towel wrapped around their heads.

town chéngzhèn [chung-jun]
  in town (zai) chéngli [(dzI) chung-lee]

tradition chuántŏng [chwahn-toong]

train huŏchē [hwor-cher]
  See TEA.

translate fānyì [fah-yee]
  could you translate that for me, please? qĭng nín bāng wŏ fānyì yíxia, hăo ma? [ching neen bahng wor fah-yee yee-syah how mah]

translation fānyì [fah-yee]

translator fānyì [fah-yee]

travel lǚxíng [lyew-sying]

travel agency lǚxíngshè [lyew-sying-shur] 旅行社

traveller's cheque lǚxíng zhīpiào [lyew-sying jur-pyow]

tree shù [shoo]
  Note the importance of getting the tones right: **shū** means 'book'!

tremendous (*excellent*) hăojíle [how-jee-ler]

trial period shìyòng qī [shur-yoong chee]

trousers kùzi [koo-dzur]

true zhēnde [jun-der]
  that's true nà shi zhēnde [nah shur jun-der]
  that's not true bú shi zhēnde

trust xìnrèn [syin-run]
  we must trust each other wŏmen yídìng yào xiānghù xìnrèn [wor-mun yee-ding yow syahng-hoo syin-run]

try shì [shur]
  we'll try wŏmen shìshi kàn [wor-mun shur-shur kahn]

Tuesday xīngqi'èr [sying-chee-er]

turnover (*of business*) yíngyè é [ying-yeh er]

twice liăngcì [lyahng-tsur]

typewriter dăzìjī [dah-dzur-jee]

typist dăzìyuán [dah-dzur-yew-ahn]

tyre lúntāi [loon-tI]

U

ugly nánkàn [nahn-kahn]

umbrella yúsăn [yew-sahn]

uncle (*father's elder brother*) bāibai [bI-bI]
  (*father's younger brother*) shūshu [shoo-shoo]
  (*mother's brother*) jiùjiu [jyoh-jyoh]

under (*spatially*) zai . . . xià [dzI . . . syah]
  (*less than*) shăoyú [show-yew]

understand dŏng [doong]
  I don't understand wŏ bù dŏng [wor boo doong]
  I understand wó dŏng le [wor doong ler]

United States Mĕiguó [may-gwor]   美国

university dàxué [dah-sonw-eh]

until dào . . . wéizhĭ [dow . . . way-jur]

unusual bù chángjiàn(de) [boo chahng-jyen(der)]

up shàng [shahng]
  this way up (*package*) cĭ duān xiàng shàng [tsur
  dwahn syahng shahng]
  sales are up xiāoshòuliàng jiànzhăng [syow-shoh-
  lyahng jyen-jahng]

upstairs lóushàng [loh-shahng]

urgent jĭnjí(de) [jin-jee(der)]

us wŏmen [wor-mun]
  that's for us nè shi géi wŏmen de [nay shur gay wor-
  mun der]
  Note that the word for 'us' is the same in Chinese as
  the word for 'we'. *See also* WE.

use yòng [yoong]
  can I use . . . ? wŏ néng yòng yíxia . . . ma? [wor nung
  yoong yee-syah . . . mah]

useful yŏuyòng(de) [yoh-yoong(der)]

usually yìbān láishuō [yee-bahn lI-shwor]

V

valid (*passport, contract*) yǒuxiào [yoh-syow]

valuable (*adjective*) zhēnguì(de) [jun-gway(der)]

vegetarian chīsùde [chur-soo-der]

VEGETARIANS
Chinese Buddhists, given the nature of their beliefs about reincarnation, were traditionally vegetarian. Temple restaurants still provide excellent vegetarian meals.

VERBS
Chinese verbs have no endings for different persons. So for example in the sentences:

> **wǒ qù**
> I go, I am going

> **nǐ qù**
> you go, you are going

> **tā qù**
> he/she goes, he/she is going

> **wǒmen qù**
> we go, we are going etc.

the verb remains unchanged. Neither does Chinese have any endings for tenses. For example:

> **wǒ qù**

could be used to mean: I go
or: I am going
or: I shall go
or: I went

This does not mean that Chinese is unable to express things that English can. Very often words such as 'yesterday', 'today', 'tomorrow' etc. will remove any possible ambiguity that there might be in any particular utterance:

> **wǒ jīntian qù**
> I'm going today
> (*literally: I today go*)

> **wǒ míngtian qù**
> I'll go tomorrow
> (*literally: I tomorrow go*)

wǒ zuótian qù de nàr
I went there yesterday
(*literally: I yesterday go (de) there*)

As you can see, all this is perfectly clear. Chinese, as opposed to European languages, demonstrates that there is no *logical* need for a separate tense at all in order to express the idea of past or future.

But Chinese does have a range of particles that can be added to verbs or to sentences in order to make distinctions of meaning (*see* PARTICLES).

When using adjectives with the verb 'to be', or when saying that something is in or at a particular place, Chinese will not use a verb at all – *see* ADJECTIVES, BE.

very hĕn [hun]
  very good hén hăo [hun how]
  very tired hĕn lèi [hun lay]
  I like it very much wó hén xĭhuān [wor hun syee-hwahn]

VERY

The meaning of **hĕn** is weaker than the English 'very' and very often when it used it does not add to the meaning of the adjective. If you want to emphasize 'very' use:

  fēicháng
  [fay-chahng]
  extremely

in place of **hĕn**.

Vietnam Yuènán [yew-eh-nahn]

Vietnamese (*adjective*) Yuènán(de) [yew-eh-nahn(der)]
  (*noun*) Yuènán ren [yew-eh-nahn run]

village cūnzi [tsoon-dzur]

visa qiānzhèng [chyen-jung]

VISA

Visas have to be obtained in advance and this should ideally be done before leaving home, although it is possible to get them in Hong Kong. Package tour and delegation members will have visas arranged for them. Businessmen, academics and people visiting friends or relatives normally need a letter of invitation from the relevant firm, college or individual before a visa can be issued. Individual tourists can now also get visas.

visit (*noun*) (*place*) cānguān [tsahn-gwahn]
(*person*) bàifǎng [bI-fahng]
we enjoyed our visit (*informal language*) wǒmen
wánrde hén hǎo [wor-mun wahnr-der hun how]
(*formal language*) wǒmende cānguān hěn chénggōng
[wor-mun-der tsahn-gwahn hun chung-goong]

voice shēngyin [shung-yin]

W

wait (*verb*) děng [dung]
    don't wait for me búyòng déng wǒ [boo-yoong dung wor]
    wait for me déngděng wǒ
    I'll wait for you wǒ déng nǐ
    I'm waiting for someone (*e.g. said to waiter*) wǒ háizai děng rén [wor hI-dzI dung run]

waiter fúwùyuán [foo-woo-yew-ahn]
    waiter! wái, fúwùyuán! [wI foo-woo-yew-ahn]

waitress nǚ fúwùyuán [nyew foo-woo-yew-ahn]

Wales Wēiěrshì [way-er-shur]

walk (*verb*) zǒu [dzoh]
    let's walk there wǒmen zǒuzhe qù ba [wor-mun dzoh-jer chyew bah]

wall qiáng [chyahng]
    the Great Wall of China Chángchéng [chahng-chung]

The Great Wall of China, which in its heyday was over 2,500 miles long, stretching from the Gobi Desert to the sea north-east of Beijing, was created by the emperor Qin Shihuang, who linked up previously existing walls and made extensions to keep out barbarians and nomads around the year 200 BC. (He is now buried near his terracotta army.) Great Wall, or in Chinese characters:

长城

has become a brand name in China for everything from machinery to toilet paper.

wallet qiánbāo [chyen-bow]
Note that the same word also means 'purse'.

want xiǎngyào [syahng-yow]
    I want . . . wǒ xiǎngyào . . . [wor syahng-yow]
    he wants . . . tā xiǎngyào . . .
    that's not what I want wǒ yào de bú shi zhè zhǒng [wor yow der boo shur jer joong]
    I don't want to go wǒ bù xiǎng qù [wor boo syahng chyew]

what do you want? nǐ yào shénme? [nee yow shun-mah]

Note that, in Chinese, you can't just say 'I don't want to'. Instead you have to repeat the verb and say what it is that you don't want to do, for example:

> **would you like to go out now? - I don't want to**
> xiànzài ní xiǎng chūqu ma? - wǒ bù xiǎng chūqu

warm nuǎnhuo [nwahn-hwor]
(*friendly etc.*) rèqíng [rer-ching]

was *see* BE.

wash (*verb*) xǐ [syee]

watch (*wrist-watch*) shóu biǎo [shoh-byow]

water shuǐ [shway]   水
a glass of water, please qǐng lái yìbēi lěng kāishuǐ
[ching ll yee-bay lung kI-shway]

WATER
Lěng kāishuǐ is cold boiled water. This is what you normally get in China, as water is not drinkable straight from the tap.
See DRINKS.

way: which is the way to . . .? dào . . . zěnme zǒu? [dow
. . . dzun-mah dzoh]

we wǒmen [wor-mun]

WE
Note that **wǒmen** is also used to mean 'us':

> **we told him**
> wǒmen gàosu tā
> **he told us**
> tā gàosu wǒmen

weak (*material*) bùjiēshi [boo-jyeh-shur]
(*person*) ruò

weather tiānqi [tyen-chee]
what weather! shénme tiānqi! [shun-mah tyen-chee]

WEATHER
It is important to realize that China is effectively a sub-continent. When you talk about its climate, it is as if you were talking about Europe, including everything from northern Scandinavia to the Algarve. Northern winters can be bitterly cold and

the visitor should do what the Chinese do and wrap up in many layers against it. Summers can be uncomfortably hot, especially in the far south, and there is often a great deal of rain. Spring and autumn are the best times for visiting China as they are relatively warm and dry times of the year.

wedding hūnlǐ [hoon-lee]
See MARRIAGE.

Wednesday xīngqisān [sying-chee-sahn]

week xīngqī [sying-chee]

WEEK

Xīngqī is the normal word for week, although a more old-fashioned form, **lǐbài** [lee-bI], is still sometimes used. Some useful phrases are:

> **one week**
> yíge xīngqī
> [yee-ger sying-chee]

> **two weeks**
> liǎngge xīngqī
> [lyahng-ger sying-chee]

> **we are staying in Shanghai for three weeks**
> wǒmen zai Shànghǎi zhù sānge xīngqī
> [wor-mun dzI shahng-hI joo sahn-ger sying-chee]

> **this week**
> zhèige xīngqī
> [jay-ger sying-chee]

> **next week**
> xià(ge) xīngqī
> [syah-ger sying-chee]

> **last week**
> shàng(ge) xīngqī
> [shahng-ger sying-chee]

> **in two weeks' time**
> liǎngge xīngqī yǐhòu
> [lyahng-ger sying-chee yee-hoh]

weekend zhōumò [joh-mor]
  at the weekend zhōumò

WEEKENDS

The Western weekend is not really observed in China. Offices and some factories work on Saturdays and are only closed on Sundays. Sunday is therefore the day most people can do their shopping, and department stores, markets and ordinary shops are all open. Factories close one day a week in rotation to reduce the demand on electricity supplies. The day off might be Monday this year and Tuesday next.

weight zhòngliàng [joong-lyahng]

welcome huānyíng [hwahn-ying]
  thank you for your very warm welcome xièxie nínde rèqíng huānyíng [syeh-syeh neen-der rer-ching hwahn-ying]
  you're welcome (*in reply to thanks*) búyòng xiè [boo-yoong syeh]

well (*in health*) (shēntǐ) hǎo [(shun-tee) how]
  not well (*in health*) bù shūfu [boo shoo-foo]
  I'm very well, thank you (*as response*) hén hǎo, xièxie [hun how syeh-syeh]
  things are going well shìqing jìnzhànde hěn shùnli [shur-ching jin-jahn-der hun shoon-lee]
  you speak English extremely well nǐde Yīngwén jiǎng de zhēn hǎo [nee-der ying-wun jyahng der jun how]

were *see* BE.

west xī [syee]
  in the west xībiānr [syee-byenr]
  in the West Xīfang [syee-fahng]

Western xīfang de [syee-fahng der]

Western-style xīshì [syee-shur]
  Western-style food xīcān [syee-tsahn]

wet shī [shur]
  (*rainy*) duōyǔ de [dwor-yew der]

what? shénme? [shun-mah]
  what is that? nà shi shénme? [nah shur shun-mah]

wheel lúnzi [loon-dzur]

when? shénme shíhòu? [shun-mah shur-hoh]
  when we arrived here wǒmen dào zhèr lái de shíhòu [wor-mun dow jur lI der shur-hoh]
  when does it start? shénme shíhòu kāishǐ? [shun-mah shur-hoh kI-shur]
  But if you want a precise answer to this question use:
    jí diǎn zhōng?
    [jee dyen-joong]
    what time?

where? năr? [nar]
   where is it? zai năr? [dzI nar]

which: which one? nă yíge? [nah yee-ger]
   which company? nă jiā gōngsi? [nah jyah goong-sur]

whisky wēishìjì [way-shur-jee]

white bái [bI]
   White is the traditional colour of mourning in China.

who? shéi? [shay]

why? wèishénme? [way-shun-mah]
   why not? wèishénme bù?

wide kuān de [kwahn der]

wife qīzi, àiren [chee-dzur, I-run]

will *see* FUTURE TENSE.

wind (*noun*) fēng [fung]

window chuānghu [chwahng-hoo]
   a window seat, please qíng gěi yíge kàochuāng de zuòwèi [ching gay yee-ger kow-chahng der dzwor-way]

wine pútaojiŭ [poo-tow-jyoh]

winter dōngtian [doong-tyen]
   in the winter dōngtian

with: with sugar jiā táng [jyah tahng]
   I don't have it with me wǒ shēnbiānr méiyǒu [wor shun-byenr may-yoh]
   If you want to say 'with' in the sense of 'accompanying someone' use **gēn . . . yìqǐ** [gun . . . yee-chee]:

      can I go with you?
      wǒ gēn nǐ yìqǐ, hǎo ma?
      [wor gun nee yee-chee how ma]

   In the sense of 'using' the Chinese is **yòng** [yoong]:

      with chopsticks/a knife
      yòng kuàizi/dāozi
      [yoong kwI-dzur/dow-dzur]

without méiyǒu [may-yoh]
   without sugar bù jiā táng [boo jyah tahng]

woman fùnǚ [foo-nyew]

WOMEN

Women's equality has been part of the credo of the Chinese revolution since before the Communist Party came to power in 1949. In principle, women have an equal place with men in society, and access to jobs and education is identical. So you will see women working in the road-mending gangs alongside men, and the manager of a factory might be a woman. In practice, Chinese women still feel there is a long way to go and there are often complaints in the press about the unequal division of household and family responsibilities.

wood (*material*) mùtou [moo-toh]

wool yángmáo [yahng-mow]

word cí [tsur]
what is the word for . . .? . . .zěnme shuō? [. . . dzun-mah shwor]

WORD ORDER
Word order in Chinese is remarkably like English in simple sentences. For example:

> **I am English**
> wǒ shi Yīngguó ren
> [wor shur ying-gwor run]

There are complications when you get into some of the more involved grammatical constructions, but the most important thing to remember is that Chinese people tend to put the topic of the sentence first and then talk about it. So, for example, if they don't like a book very much, they might say:

> **zhèiběn shū wǒ bú tài xǐhuān**
> [jay-bun shoo wor boo tI syee-hwahn]
> this book I not much like

If you don't put the topic first, they will be on tenterhooks waiting to hear what you are talking about.

The other important point about word order is that expressions of place and time tend to come towards the beginning of the sentence:

> **wǒ míngtian qù Běijīng**
> [wor ming-tyen chyew bay-jing]
> I am going to Beijing tomorrow
> (*literally: I tomorrow go Beijing*)

> **tā zai Shànghǎi gōngzuò**
> [tah dzI shahng-hI goong-dzwor]
> he works in Shanghai
> (*literally: he in Shanghai works*)

work (*noun*) gōngzuò [goong-dzwor]
   it's a lot of work zhè hěn fèigōng [jay hun fay-goong]
   it's not working (*machine etc.*) zhè bù gōngzuò le [jay
   boo goong-dzwor ler]

worry: don't worry bié zháojí [byeh jow-jee]

worse gènghuài [gung-hI]

write xiě [syeh]
   could you write it down? máfan nín bǎ tā xiě xiàlai,
   hǎo ma? [mah-fahn neen bah tah syeh syah-lI how
   mah]

writing: Chinese writing hànzì [hahn-dzur]
   See CHARACTERS.

wrong cuò [tswor]
   is something wrong? zěmele? [dzun-mer-ler]

Y

Yangzi River Cháng jiāng [chahng jyahng]

yawn (*noun*) hāqiàn [hah-chyen]

year nián [nyen]

YEAR

Some useful phrases are:

> **last year**
> qùnián
> [chyew-nyen]
>
> **this year**
> jīnnián
> [jin-nyen]
>
> **next year**
> míngnián
> [ming-nyen]

Nián, like the word **tiān**, day, is considered to be a classifier in its own right, so you do not need to add an extra classifier when you are counting:

> **three years**
> sān nián

A year in school or college is **niánjí** [nyen-jee]:

> **they are third-year students**
> tāmen shi sān niánjí xuésheng

See CALENDAR.

yellow huáng [hwahng]

Yellow River Huáng hé [hwahng her]

yes shìde [shur-der]
   yes, please hǎo, xièxie [how syeh-syeh]

YES

There is no one word for 'yes' (or indeed 'no') in Chinese. One way of saying 'yes' is to use the verb which the speaker used in the question which he/she just asked. For example:

> **is he Chinese?**
> tā shi Zhōngguo ren ma?
> [tah shur joong-gwor run ma]
> (*literally: he is Chinese person (question word)*)

yes, he is
shì
[shur]

do you like China?
ní xǐhuān Zhōngguo ma?
[nee syee-hwahn joong-gwor mah]

yes, I do
xǐhuān
[syee-hwahn]
(*literally: I like*)

If you want to use the word 'yes' to agree with what someone has said, you can also use:

duì (or duìle)
[dway-ler]

which means:

correct

are you learning Chinese?
nǐ zai xué Zhōngwen ma?
[nee dzI syew-eh joong-wun mah]

yes, I am
duì
[dway]

If you are happy to go along with a suggestion someone has made, you can say:

xíng (or hǎo)
[sying, how]
OK

shall we have a drink?
wǒmen hē diǎnr shénme ba?
[wor-mun her dyenr shun-mah bah]

yes
xíng (or hǎo)

yesterday zuótian [dzwor-tyen]
　the day before yesterday qiántiān [chyen-tyen]

yet: not yet hái méiyou . . . [hI may-yoh]
　has he come yet? tā láile ma? [tah lI ler mah]

yoghurt suānnǎi [swahn-nI]

YOGHURT

This is popular in Beijing and is sold at kiosks from breakfast time onwards. It is ladled into jars or pots which people bring to the kiosk often in a small, home-made wooden carrying frame.

you nǐ [nee]
　　(*politer*) nín [neen]
　　(*plural*) nǐmen [nee-mun]
　　(*politer*) nínmen [neen-mun]

YOU

Nǐ is the standard way of addressing someone as
'you', with **nín** being a politer version. This does not
correspond to the polite forms in French or German
but is more similar to what is expressed by the
difference between, for example, 'can you' and
'could you' in English:

> **can you write it down?**
> máfan nǐ ba tā xiě xiàlai, hǎo ma?

> **could you write it down?**
> máfan nǐn ba tā xiě xiàlai, hǎo ma?

young niánqīng [nyen-ching]

your (*singular*) nǐde [nee-der]
　　(*politer*) nínde [neen-der]
　　(*plural*) nǐmende [nee-mun-der]
　　(*politer*) nínmende [neen-mun-der]
　　is that your pen? nà shi bú shi nǐde gāngbǐ? [nah
　　shur boo shur nee-der gahng-bee]
　　your rooms nǐmende fángjiān [nee-mun-der fahng-
　　jyen]

yours nǐde [nee-der]
　　The Chinese words for 'yours' are the same as the
　　words for 'your' (*see* YOUR).

Z

zero líng
zip lāliàn [lah-lyen]

NOTES

NOTES

NOTES

NOTES

NOTES